TWO BEATRIX POTTER PLAYS

Adrian Mitchell

JEMIMA PUDDLE-DUCK AND HER FRIENDS

and

PETER RABBIT AND HIS FRIENDS

based on the stories of Beatrix Potter

First published in 2005 by Oberon Books Ltd
521 Caledonian Road, London N7 9RH
Tel: 020 7607 3637 / Fax: 020 7607 3629
e-mail: oberon.books@btinternet.com
www.oberonbooks.com

Contents

THE GREAT BEATRIX POTTER

I first met the wonderful stories and pictures of Beatrix Potter when I was two or three. My mother and father took turns to read to me and my big brother Jimmy every single night. And some of our first stories were about Jeremy Fisher the foolhardy frog, the magical but down-to-earth Mrs Tiggy-Winkle and the mischievous Peter Rabbit himself. The stories came in small, bright books which were just the right size for a small boy's grubby hands.

Later I read the same stories (with the same pictures) to my own children. And now I find myself reading them to my amazing grandchildren. This could go on for ever, I suppose. But however often I read them or listen to them, I never get bored. Why not? Because Beatrix Potter was one of the best writers who ever lived. The words of her stories are funny, clever and full of surprises. Her animal characters are often silly or naughty, just like us, but they are great company, enjoying their adventures in the beautiful countryside which still exists in parts of England. They are lovingly told, but never sentimental. There are some dark and frightening moments in some of the stories – when Jemima Puddle-Duck is meets the sinister gentleman with sandy whiskers and when the two villainous rats, Samuel Whiskers and Anna Maria, try to turn Tom Kitten into a roly-poly pudding.

Some years ago I went to the Unicorn Theatre for Children and Warne, Beatrix Potter's publishers, with a plan. I wanted to write three Beatrix Potter plays, each of them containing four of her stories. We started with *Tom Kitten and His Friends* (published by Samuel French). Stephen McNeff, a fine musician/magician, wrote the music for the songs. Everybody liked the play and Stephen and I went on to write *Jemima Puddle-Duck and Her Friends* and *Peter Rabbit and His Friends*. The reviews were excellent, the Unicorn Theatre was always full, in London and on tour, and children often came out dancing and singing the songs. So now there are three plays, containing four stories each. Somebody said to me: 'But what do these stories teach children?' I said: They teach children and adults to understand and love the English language and animals and the countryside. But they teach with a light heart, through stories which are odd and exciting and funny. But the main reason I wrote these plays was to entertain my grandchildren and to have fun.

I'd like to dedicate all the plays – my 'Ring Cycle' – to the Unicorn Theatre for Children in its new home in London. And to add my wish that every town in England which has a League Football Club should also have a theatre for children.

Adrian Mitchell, 2004

JEMIMA PUDDLE-DUCK
AND HER FRIENDS

Characters

BEATRIX POTTER

JEMIMA PUDDLE-DUCK

FARMER'S WIFE

REBECCAH PUDDLE-DUCK

FOX

KEP
a collie dog

TWO BEAGLE PUPPIES

FOUR DUCKLINGS

SQUIRREL NUTKIN

TWINKLEBERRY
Nutkin's brother

MOSSTAIL
female leader of the Squirrels

SQUIRRELS

OLD BROWN
an owl

JEREMY FISHER
a frog

MRS SNAIL

JACK SHARP
a stickleback

TROUT

SIR ISAAC NEWTON
a newt

MR ALDERMAN PTOLEMY
tortoise

TABITHA TWITCHIT
a motherly cat

MISS MOPPET
MITTENS
TOM KITTEN
her kittens

MRS RIBBY
her cousin

SAMUEL WHISKERS
a rat

ANNA MARIA
another rat, married to Samuel

SPIDER

JOHN JOINER
a canine carpenter

FARMER POTATOES

Jemima Puddle-Duck and Her Friends was first staged by the Unicorn Theatre for Children at the Arts Theatre on 11 October 1998. The company were:

KEP / OLD BROWN / JEREMY FISHER / MRS RIBBY, Mark Bowden

JEMIMA PUDDLE-DUCK / SQUIRREL / MR ALDERMAN PTOLEMY TORTOISE / TABITHA TWITCHIT, Andrea Francis

BEAGLE PUPPY / TWINKLEBERRY / MITTENS / ANNA MARIA, Bethan Morgan

BEAGLE PUPPY / SQUIRREL NUTKIN / MOPPET / SAMUEL WHISKERS, Rosalind Paul

FOX / SQUIRREL / JOHN JOINER / SIR ISAAC NEWTON, Jonathan Savage

BEATRIX POTTER, Jane Tucker

(All other characters played by members of the cast.)

Director Tony Graham

Composer and Music Director Stephen McNeff

Designer Sophia Lovell Smith

Lighting Designer Gerry Jenkinson

Movement Director Jenny Weston

ACT ONE

Curtain up on a stage with a piano and piano-stool. The actress who will play BEATRIX POTTER is at the piano, playing one of the songs from the show. She wears modern, everyday clothes. She notices the audience, gets up and goes to the front of the stage to greet them.

BEATRIX: Good morning/Good afternoon.
   (She waits for a response from the audience.)
   This is what we call the stage of our theatre. The stage is
   where we act stories and sing songs for you. Can you all
   see me? You'll see me better if we brighten the lights on
   the stage –
   (BEATRIX POTTER raises her hand and the stage lights brighten.)
   And now we can turn out the lights on your seats.
   (Lights down gradually in auditorium as BEATRIX POTTER lowers her hand.)
   That's better. We're ready to begin.
   Once upon a time there was a woman called Beatrix
   Potter. She loved animals. She painted pictures of
   animals and wrote little books about their adventures.
   We're going to tell you some of those stories. So I'm
   going to dress up as Beatrix Potter. *(She takes clothes from
   a basket beside the piano.)* She liked to wear a long skirt
   like this one. *(She fastens a skirt round her waist.)* Fasten it
   at the side. And a little dark jacket just as soft a kitten.
   (Putting on the jacket.) And on top of her head, what do
   you think she wore? *(Pause.)* That's right – she wore a hat
   like this. *(Puts on the hat.)* Now I'm Beatrix Potter. I'm
   going to sing you a song about the first story. *(She sits at
   the piano, and plays. She sings.)*
      I had a cat and the cat pleased me,
      I fed my cat by yonder tree;
      Cat goes fiddle-i-fee.
   No, I'll save my cat story for later.
      I had a duck and the duck pleased me,
      I fed my duck by yonder tree;

Duck goes quack, quack,
Cat goes fiddle-i-fee!

Yes. I'll start with a duck story. Long ago I lived in a farm in the hills. And I had a real duck called Jemima Puddle-Duck. But I knew a little girl called Mollie who used to call her Jemima Pudding Duck. And this is The Tale of Jemima Puddle-Duck.

(*Lights change.*)

Jemima was annoyed because the farmer's wife would not let her hatch her own eggs. She always took the eggs away from Jemima.

(*Enter JEMIMA.*)

JEMIMA: (*Sings.*)

Pit pat paddle pat!
Pit pat waddle pat!
Pit pat paddle pat!
Pit pat waddle pat!
I'm Jemima Puddle-Duck.
I'm Jemima Puddle-Duck.
Pit pat paddle pat!
Pit pat waddle pat!

BEATRIX: Jemima would find a warm little corner of the farmyard – like this:

JEMIMA: This looks like a good place to lay eggs. The farmer's wife will never find them. I'm ready to lay some eggs. (*JEMIMA wiggles and lays an egg. Then another. Then another. She stands, shakes her tail, turns and looks at the eggs.*) What sweet little eggs!

BEATRIX: I'll be the farmer's wife. She always wears a white apron like this. (*Puts on an apron.*)

JEMIMA: What dear little eggs!

(*BEATRIX POTTER as FARMER'S WIFE approaches with basket.*

JEMIMA crouches down over the eggs.)

JEMIMA: (*Hopefully.*) She won't see me. She won't see me.

FARMER'S WIFE: Good morning, Jemima Puddle-Duck.

JEMIMA: (*Shrugging.*) O – good morning!

FARMER'S WIFE: What are you doing all scrunched up in the corner, Jemima?

JEMIMA: Just resting, you know.

FARMER'S WIFE: Yes, I know. Resting after laying me
some lovely fresh eggs. (*She pushes JEMIMA to one side.*)
Fresh eggs for the market – one, two, three! (*Puts them in
her basket.*) Thank you very much, Jemima Puddle-Duck!
(*Exit FARMER'S WIFE.*)

JEMIMA: But I wanted to sit on those eggs and keep them
warm and hatch them out into darling little ducklings!
(*Wails.*) She's done it again! She's done it again!
(*MRS REBECCAH PUDDLE-DUCK hurries up.*)

REBECCAH: (*Sings.*)

> **Pit pat paddle pat!**
> **Pit pat waddle pat!**
> **Pit pat paddle pat!**
> **Pit pat waddle pat!**
> **I'm Rebeccah Puddle-Duck.**
> **I'm Rebeccah Puddle-Duck.**
> **Pit pat paddle pat!**
> **Pit pat waddle pat!**

REBECCAH: What's the matter, Jemima? Why are you
making such a racket with your quacking?

JEMIMA: Oh Rebeccah, it's the Farmer's Wife. She won't
let me hatch my lovely eggs.

REBECCAH: You haven't the patience to sit on a nest for
twenty-eight days. You'd let your eggs go cold; you
know you would.

JEMIMA: They're my eggs. I'll hatch them all by myself.

REBECCAH: I don't think you will, Jemima Puddle-Duck

JEMIMA: Oh yes I will, Rebeccah Puddle-Duck. I'll hide
them very cleverly.

REBECCAH: The Farmer's Wife is cleverer than you.

JEMIMA: I've made up my mind. I shall go on a journey
and make a nest a long way from the farm.

REBECCAH: You take care, Jemima. It's much safer on the
farm.

JEMIMA: Not for my eggs. I'm off to find a new nest.
(*She puts on a shawl and a blue poke bonnet.*)

BEATRIX: Jemima Puddle-Duck set off on a fine spring afternoon along the cart-track that leads over the hill. She was wearing a shawl and a poke bonnet.

JEMIMA: (*Sings.*)

> **Pit pat paddle pat!**
> **Pit pat waddle pat!**
> **Pit pat paddle pat!**
> **Pit pat paddle pat!**

(*Puffed.*) Quack – it's a steep old hill. This must be the top. I can see a nice green wood in the distance. It looks a safe quiet spot. Just right for my new nest. I'll waddle down there. No, it would be much quicker to fly. But I'm not used to flying. Perhaps if I start by running downhill and flapping my shawl and then jumping off into the air? Would I fly? I'll try!

(*JEMIMA runs, flapping her shawl and begins to fly.*)

That was a good start. Now I'm flying beautifully.

(*Sings.*)

> **With my feathery wings**
> **And my feathery tail**
> **All over the beautiful world I sail**
> **Skimming along the tree-tops**
> **Up in the April sky.**
> **I feel like a cloud**
> **And I'm quacking aloud**
> **It's a wonderful thing to fly!**
> **With my feathery wings**
> **And my feathery tail**
> **All over the beautiful world I sail.**
> **Floating above the meadows**
> **Nobody's flown so high.**
> **I'm gliding along**
> **With a puddle-duck song –**
> **It's a wonderful thing to fly!**

I can see an open place down there in the middle of the wood. Just right for a graceful landing.

(*JEMIMA lands clumsily, clambers to her feet and begins to waddle about.*)

(*Sings.*)
> **Pit pat paddle pat!**
> **Pit pat waddle pat!**

Now where can I find dry nesting place? I like the tree-stump by those tall fox-gloves. Oh, but who's that? An elegantly dressed gentleman, reading a newspaper.
(*A FOX keeps reading his newspaper as he sits in his blue baggy suit, cross-legged, sitting on his long bushy tail.*)
Quack? Quack?
(*The FOX looks over the top of his newspaper and looks curiously at JEMIMA.*)

FOX: Madam, have you lost your way?

JEMIMA: Oh you are very polite, sir. (*To audience.*) And very handsome, too. No, I haven't lost my way. I am looking for a clean, dry place for a nest.

FOX: (*Folding up his newspaper and putting it in his coat-tail pocket.*) Ah! Is that so? Indeed!

JEMIMA: I'm going to hatch my own eggs.

FOX: Of course you are, madam. I'm sure you can nest in my woodshed. Very comfortable – I have a sackful of feathers in there.

JEMIMA: I couldn't trouble you –

FOX: Oh my dear madam, you'll be in nobody's way. You may sit there as long as you like. Let me show you.
(*The FOX leads JEMIMA towards a hut made of sticks and turf, with two broken buckets on the roof by way of a chimney.*)
This is my summer house. You would not find my earth – I mean my winter home – so convenient.
(*The FOX opens the door and shows JEMIMA in, sniggering to himself under his breath. She suspects nothing.*)

JEMIMA: It's all full of feathers! They nearly choke you. Ooh, but they're very soft and comfortable. I can make a nest here without any trouble at all.

FOX: (*Sitting down and reading his newspaper.*) I'm so glad it suits you.

JEMIMA: So many feathers! Where do they all come from?

FOX: Who knows? Lots of feathers in the wood, you know! Lots of feathers!

JEMIMA: Well I must hurry home to my farmyard for the night.

FOX: Must you go? So soon? You haven't even told me your name.

JEMIMA: I am Jemima Puddle-Duck.

FOX: Well, Jemima, I promise to take great care of your new nest till you come back tomorrow. I'm so fond of eggs and ducklings.

BEATRIX: Jemima Puddle-Duck came every afternoon to visit the handsome gentleman. She laid nine eggs in the nest. They were greeny white and very large.

(*The FOX inspects eggs carefully.*)

The foxy gentleman admired them immensely. He used to turn them over and count them when Jemima was not there.

JEMIMA: (*Arriving.*) What are you doing, sir, with my eggs?

FOX: I was simply counting them, my dear madam. (*Sings.*)

One egg two eggs three eggs four
Five eggs six eggs seven eggs more
Eight eggs nine eggs in the nest
Which little egg do you love best?

(*The FOX and JEMIMA sing and dance.*)

One egg two eggs three eggs four
Five eggs six eggs seven eggs more
Eight eggs nine eggs in the nest
Which little egg do you love best?

JEMIMA: Tomorrow I am going to begin to sit on my eggs. I will bring a bag of corn with me, so I need never leave my nest until the eggs are hatched. They might catch cold.

FOX: Madam, don't trouble to bring any corn. I'll give you a sack of oats. And when your eggs are hatched, we shall have nine little ducklings!

FOX: (*Sings.*)

One duck two ducks three ducks four
Five ducks six ducks seven ducks more
Eight ducks nine ducks out of their eggs
Nine little ducks on wobbly legs!

(The FOX and JEMIMA sing and dance.)
> **One duck two ducks three ducks four**
> **Five ducks six ducks seven ducks more**
> **Eight ducks nine ducks out of their eggs**
> **Nine little ducks on wobbly legs!**

FOX: But before you begin sitting on your eggs, I would like to give you a treat. Let's have a dinner-party all to ourselves.

JEMIMA: A dinner-party! I've never been to a dinner-party.

FOX: May I ask you to pick some herbs from the garden of the farm so I can make an omelette? Sage and thyme, and mint and two onions. And some parsley. I will provide lard for the stuff – lard for the omelette.

BEATRIX: Jemima Puddle-Duck was a simpleton. Not even the mention of omelette or sage and onions made her suspicious. But we know that omelettes are made with eggs. And sage and onions are used to make the stuffing for – roast duck! Jemima waddled down to the farm-garden, nibbling off snippets of all the different herbs which are used for stuffing roast duck.

JEMIMA: Now I'll pop into the kitchen and find a couple of onions.

BEATRIX: But Kep, the faithful collie dog, met her coming out of the kitchen.

(KEP, a handsome brown and white sheepdog, confronts her.)

KEP: *(Firmly, but kindly.)* What are you doing with those onions? Where do you go every afternoon by yourself, Jemima Puddle-Duck?

JEMIMA: *(Nervously.)* I wanted to find a safe quiet place to hatch my eggs. And in the wood I met a kind gentleman who let me make a nest in his summer house.

KEP: What kind of summer house?

JEMIMA: Very comfortable, all full of feathers.

KEP: Full of feathers? I see. And this kind gentleman, what does he look like?

JEMIMA: Well, he's elegantly dressed. And very handsome. With a long bushy tail. And sandy whiskers.

KEP: And pointy ears that stand up and a sharp black nose?

JEMIMA: Do you know him?

KEP: I think so. Now this summer house – where is it?

JEMIMA: Right in the middle of the wood.

KEP: I see.

BEATRIX: Then Kep trotted down to the village. He went to look for two fox-hound puppies who were out for a walk.

(KEP approaches two beagle PUPPIES. They sniff each other and begin to plot.)

Jemima Puddle-Duck went up the cart-road for the last time, on a sunny afternoon. She carried bunches of herbs and two onions in a bag. She flew over the wood and alighted opposite the house of the bushy long-tailed gentleman.

(The FOX sits on a log. He sniffs the air and glances uneasily around the wood. He jumps when JEMIMA lands beside him.)

FOX: *(Abruptly.)* Come into the house as soon as you have looked at your eggs. Give me the herbs for the omelette. Be sharp!

JEMIMA: Here you are.

(She gives him the herbs and goes to look at her eggs.
KEP comes up and locks her in the summer house.)

Quack! Quack! Somebody's locked me in!

(FOX turns to see KEP and the two PUPPIES approaching.)

FOX: Now you must understand, gentlemen, I was merely protecting Mrs Puddle-Duck from the dangers of the wood –

(But KEP and the two PUPPIES are snarling and moving in on him.
The FOX takes to his heels and a wonderful chase ensues to riotous music and barking, baying, growls and howls.)

BEATRIX: And nothing more was ever seen of that foxy-whiskered gentleman.

(KEP opens the door to the summer house.
JEMIMA waddles out.)

JEMIMA: Kep, what are you doing here?

BEATRIX: Unfortunately the puppies rushed in and
gobbled up all the eggs before Kep could stop them. Kep
had a bite on his ear, and both the puppies were limping.
They took Jemima Puddle-Duck home in tears because
of those eggs. She laid some more in June. She was
allowed to keep them for herself. But only four of them
hatched. Jemima Puddle-Duck said that was because of
her nerves; but she always had been a bad sitter.
(*JEMIMA marches about with four little yellow
DUCKLINGS – these may be wooden ducklings on wheels
which nod their heads – that sort of thing – but we should
hear their voices from offstage actors.*)

JEMIMA & DUCKLINGS: (*Sing.*)

    Pit pat paddle pat!
    Pit pat waddle pat!
    Pit pat paddle pat!
    Pit pat waddle pat!
    We are the Puddle-ducks.
    We are the Puddle-ducks.
    Pit pat paddle pat!
    Pit pat waddle pat!

BEATRIX: And that is the end of the Tale of Jemima
Puddle-Duck. (*Sings.*)

    I had a cat and the cat pleased me
    I fed my cat by yonder tree;
    Cat goes fiddle-i-fee.
    I had a duck and the duck pleased me
    I fed my duck by yonder tree;
    Duck goes quack quack,
    Cat goes fiddle-i-fee.
    I had a squirrel and the squirrel pleased me
    I fed my squirrel by yonder tree;
    Squirrel goes chatter chatter,
    Duck goes quack quack,
    Cat goes fiddle-i-fee.

Yes, my next story is about squirrels. One day I saw a
most comical little red squirrel in the woods. His tail
was only an inch long, but he was so cheeky, he

chattered and clattered and threw down acorns onto my head. I believe that his name was Nutkin and that he had a brother called Twinkleberry, and this is the story about how he lost his tail – The Tale of Squirrel Nutkin. So this is a tale about a tail.

(*Enter NUTKIN. He is a cheeky and bouncy red squirrel. He bows to the audience and swirls his tail proudly.*)

NUTKIN: I am Squirrel Nutkin. (*Sings.*)

> **I'm a red squirrel**
> **And I live in a tree**
> **You'll never see a finer**
> **Squirrel than me**
> **I'm all red and furry**
> **From my head to my toes**
> **And I wave my tail**
> **And I wrinkle my nose.**

I have a brother called Twinkleberry.

(*TWINKLEBERRY appears beside NUTKIN.*)

TWINKLEBERRY: (*Sings.*)

> **I'm another red squirrel**
> **And I live in a tree**
> **You'll never see a finer**
> **Squirrel than me –**

NUTKIN: (*Sings.*)

> **Except me!**

NUTKIN & TWINKLEBERRY: (*Sing.*)

> **We're all red and furry**
> **From our head to our toeses**
> **And we wave our tails**
> **And we wrinkle our noses.**

NUTKIN: Twinkleberry and I have many cousins.

TWINKLEBERRY: A great many cousins.

NUTKIN & TWINKLEBERRY: Dozens of cousins!

(*Many other SQUIRRELS emerge – as many as possible, whether they are played by actors or puppets.*)

SQUIRRELS: (*Sing.*)

> **Oh we're all red squirrels**
> **And we live in a tree**

You'll never see finer
Squirrels than we –
NUTKIN: (*Sings.*)
Except me!
SQUIRRELS: (*Sing.*)
We're all red and furry
From our head to our toeses
And we wave our tails
And we wrinkle our noses.
NUTKIN: And we live in a wood –
TWINKLEBERRY: A very good wood –
NUTKIN: We live in a wood at the edge of a lake.
TWINKLEBERRY: What's a lake, Nutkin?
NUTKIN: For heaven's sake – down there – that's a lake.
TWINKLEBERRY: Oh, a lake is a puddle.
NUTKIN: No, no, no, no, no, no – yes. Well. A lake is a
    big, huge, enormous, giant kind of puddle.
TWINKLEBERRY: Is a lake wetter than a puddle?
NUTKIN: (*Chewing his tail in agonising thought.*) Er – yes. A
    lake is wetter than a puddle because there is more lake
    than puddle.
TWINKLEBERRY: Let me sit down to think about that.
    (*TWINKLEBERRY, who has a curious mind but is not the*
    brightest squirrel in the world, sits down to ponder the pond/
    lake question.)
    (*MOSSTAIL, a senior squirrel with grey in her fur, who*
    may be played by the actress who plays BEATRIX POTTER,
    has been listening to NUTKIN and TWINKLEBERRY
    critically.)
MOSSTAIL: (*Pushing NUTKIN aside and addresses audience.*)
    Pay no attention to Nutkin. He is a very young and
    cheeky squirrel. As you shall see.
NUTKIN: Oh, let me tell the story, Mosstail.
MOSSTAIL: I am the leader of the squirrels, so I shall tell
    the story. In the middle of our lake there is an island.
    The island is covered with trees and nut bushes. And in
    that wood stands a hollow oak-tree, which is the house of
    an owl who is called Old Mr Brown.

(*Lights up on OLD BROWN, large owl perching on his oak-tree home.*

The tree has dark wood door at the bottom and a circular hollow higher up.)

OLD BROWN: (*Sings.*)
> I sleep all day
> In the golden sun
> While you little animals
> Are having fun
> But when the moon comes up
> And the day is done
> All you little animals
> Had better run
> For I can swoop
> Woop! Woop!
> To catch mice and squirrels to put in my soup
> So when the moon comes up
> And the day is done
> All you little animals
> Had better run.

Remember my name – Old Brown!

MOSSTAIL: It's autumn. So it's time for every good squirrel to make a raft and travel across the lake to Owl Island.

TWINKLEBERRY: Why do we go to Owl Island? My mother told me to beware of owls. My uncle Munkaduke was gobbled up by an owl.

NUTKIN: Nuts!

TWINKLEBERRY: (*Offended.*) What did you say?

NUTKIN: Nuts! We go to Owl Island to collect nuts.

(*SQUIRRELS all bring on little rafts, probably on wheels, and sticks to use as poles or paddles.*)

SQUIRRELS: (*Sing.*)
> In autumn time
> When the nuts are ripe
> And the hazel bushes
> Are golden and green
> We all run down

To the edge of the lake
Where the waters
Are clear and clean
On our little rafts
We paddle away
Past the quacking waterfowl
And we spread out our tails
As bushy red sails
And the autumn breeze
Blows us to the trees
On the island of the owl.

(*This song should be slow and should accompany a stage image of the squirrels sailing to the island. By the end they should have landed on the island and, while NUTKIN is fooling around, MOSSTAIL should be rallying them.*)

MOSSTAIL: My fellow-squirrels, hush! We are now on the shores of Owl Island. We have a mission here, a mission to gather –

NUTKIN: Nuts!

MOSSTAIL: Shhhh! You all have your little sacks?

SQUIRRELS: Yes! Sacks! (*Holding up sacks.*)

MOSSTAIL: And have we brought a present of three fat mice as a present for Old Brown the Owl?

SQUIRRELS: Yes! Present! (*Holding up three mice by their tails.*)

MOSSTAIL: Lay the mice on the stone in front of Old Brown's doorway.

(*OLD BROWN steps out on to his doorstep and regards the squirrels through narrowed eyes.*
The SQUIRRELS each, except NUTKIN, bow deeply to him.
They lay the mice at OLD BROWN's feet.)

MOSSTAIL: Old Mr Brown, will you allow us to gather nuts upon your island?

SQUIRRELS: (*In unison.*) Old Mr Brown, will you allow us to gather nuts upon your island?

MOSSTAIL: Now Nutkin, as I have told you, was very young and cheeky. He was very fond of riddles. Do you know what a riddle is?

TWINKLEBERRY: Yes, yes! A riddle is when you go like this.

(*TWINKLEBERRY wriggles.*)

MOSSTAIL: No, Twinkleberry. A riddle is not when you go like this.

(*MOSSTAIL wriggles.*)

A riddle is when you ask a question which is a puzzle. And the answer is a trick. Like – why did the squirrel cross the lake?

NUTKIN: To get to the other side! Oh I love riddles. Old Brown, Old Brown, listen to my riddle! (*Sings.*)

Riddle me, riddle me, rot-tot-tote!

A little wee man, in a red red coat!

A staff in his hand, and a stone in his throat;

If you'll tell me this riddle, I'll give you a groat.

(*OLD BROWN takes no notice. He shuts his eyes and pretends to sleep.*)

MOSSTAIL: Now Nutkin's riddle is as old as the hills. Do you know the answer?

(*Wait for answer.*

MOSSTAIL opens a paw to show a large cherry with a stalk.)

That's right – a cherry – a little man in a red coat. A staff in his hand and a stone in his throat. But Mr Brown did not care for riddles.

TWINKLEBERRY: Old Brown seemed to be fast asleep. So we all filled our little sacks with nuts and sailed away home in the evening.

MOSSTAIL: Next morning we all came back.

(*SQUIRRELS stand in front of OLD BROWN's doorway again.*)

MOSSTAIL: Who has brought a present for Old Brown today?

TWINKLEBERRY: I have brought a present. A fine fat mole!

MOSSTAIL: Then lay it on the stone.

(*TWINKLEBERRY nervously lays the mole on the stone in front of OLD BROWN's doorway.*

OLD BROWN regards the squirrels through narrowed eyes.

The SQUIRRELS, all except NUTKIN, bow deeply to him.)

MOSSTAIL: Old Mr Brown, will you allow us to gather some more nuts?

SQUIRRELS: (*In unison.*) Old Mr Brown, will you allow us to gather some more nuts?

NUTKIN: I've got another riddle! I've got another riddle. (*He sings as he dances up and down, tickling OLD BROWN with a nettle.*)

> **Old Mr B! Riddle-me-ree!**
> **Hitty pitty within the wall,**
> **Hitty pitty without the wall;**
> **It you touch hitty pitty,**
> **Hitty pitty will bite you!**

(*OLD BROWN wakes up with a snort and carries the mole into his house.*)

TWINKLEBERRY: What's the answer to that riddle, Nutkin?

(*Pause, in case audience knows.*)

NUTKIN: (*Teasing TWINKLEBERRY with the nettle.*) A stinging nettle! If you touch Hitty Pitty, Hitty Pitty will bite you!

TWINKLEBERRY: Ouch! I don't like that one.

MOSSTAIL: That's enough of your cheekiness, Nutkin. Come and help. We've all got to fill our sacks with nuts. (*MOSSTAIL and other SQUIRRELS resume hunt for nuts.*)

NUTKIN: (*To audience.*) I don't feel like gathering nuts today. Here are some nice little round oak apples. I think I'll stay here and play marbles with them. I can keep watch on Old Mr Brown's front door. (*Playing marbles.*) That was a good one!

MOSSTAIL: On the third day all of us squirrels got up very early and went fishing. We caught seven fat minnows as a present for Old Mr Brown. We paddled over the lake and landed under a crooked chestnut tree on Owl Island.

TWINKLEBERRY: I'm carrying a nice fat minnow.

SQUIRRELS: We're all carrying nice fat minnows.

NUTKIN: I'm not carrying a nice fat minnow.

MOSSTAIL: That's because your manners are so bad. Fancy bringing no present at all.

NUTKIN: Oh, I've brought a present. I always bring a present. But my present is a nice fat riddle.
(*NUTKIN dances up to OLD BROWN.*)
NUTKIN: Here's another riddle, Old Brown!
(*Sings.*)
> **A house full, a hole full!**
> **And you cannot gather a bowl-full!**

TWINKLEBERRY: Is it soup?
NUTKIN: You can't have a house full of soup! It's smoke – you can't gather a bowl-full of smoke, can you?
OLD BROWN: I take no interest in riddles. Not even when the answer is provided.
MOSSTAIL: On the fourth day we brought a present of six fat beetles, which were good as plums in a plum-pudding for Old Mr Brown. Each beetle was wrapped up carefully in a dock-leaf, fastened with a pine-needle pin.
(*SQUIRRELS lay the beetles on the stone as OLD BROWN watches.*)
But young Nutkin was as rude as ever and sang another of his silly riddles.
NUTKIN: (*Sings to OLD BROWN.*)
> **Old Mr B! Riddle-me-ree**
> **Flour of England, fruit of Spain,**
> **Met together in a shower of rain;**
> **Put in a bag tied round with a string,**
> **If you'll tell me this riddle, I'll give you a ring!**

NUTKIN: He'll never guess – he's too old and sleepy. The answer is – Christmas pudding!
OLD BROWN: I take no interest in riddles. Even riddles about food. Riddles annoy me. I shall go indoors and eat my beetles.
(*OLD BROWN goes into his tree with his beetles.*)
MOSSTAIL: I wouldn't make fun of Old Mr Brown if I were you, Squirrel Nutkin.
NUTKIN: Well, you're not me, are you, Old Mosstail?
MOSSTAIL: On the fifth day we brought a present of wild honey.

TWINKLEBERRY: It was so sweet and sticky that we licked our fingers as we put it down upon the stone.
(*SQUIRRELS put down a honeycomb in front of OLD BROWN.*)

NUTKIN: They stole that honeycomb out of a bumble bee's nest on the tippity top of the hill. So I sang Old Brown a riddle about a bumble bee!

NUTKIN: (S*kips up and down, singing.*)
Hum-a-bum! Buzz! Buzz! Hum-a-bum buzz!
As I went over tipple-tine
I met a flock of bonny swine;
Some yellow-nacked, some yellow-backed!
They were the very bonniest swine
That e'er went over tipple-tine.

OLD BROWN: I have already told you my opinion of riddles. I will now tell you my opinion of you, small squirrel. You are impudent and rude and ridiculous. I am now going to eat my honeycomb.

MOSSTAIL: One day you'll go too far, Nutkin.

TWINKLEBERRY: Come and help us gather nuts.

NUTKIN: No thanks, I've got a better idea. I'll play ninepins with a crab apple and green fir cones.
(*NUTKIN demonstrates.*)
Oh, nice shot, sir!

MOSSTAIL: (*To audience.*) On the sixth day, which was Saturday, we came again for the last time. This time we brought a new-laid egg in a little rush basket as a last parting present for Old Mr Brown.
(*SQUIRRELS place the egg reverently at OLD BROWN's feet.*)

OLD BROWN: Now I do take an interest in eggs.

NUTKIN: (*Rushing up.*) What about sunbeams? You don't like the daytime much do you, old owly? Here's a sunbeam riddle: (*Sings.*)
Old Mr B! Old Mr B!
Hickamore, hackamore, on the king's kitchen door;
All the king's horses, and all the king's men,
Couldn't drive hickamore, hackamore,
Off the king's kitchen door.

MOSSTAIL: (*As NUTKIN acts it out.*) Then Nutkin tried to dance like a sunbeam. And he took a running jump –

TWINKLEBERRY: Right onto the head of Old Brown.

MOSSTAIL: Then all at once –

TWINKLEBERRY: There was a flutterment and a scufflement –

MOSSTAIL: And a loud Squeak!

TWINKLEBERRY: And all the squirrels except Nutkin scuttered away into the bushes.

MOSSTAIL: When we came back –

TWINKLEBERRY: Very cautiously, peeping round the tree –

MOSSTAIL: There was Old Mr Brown sitting on his doorstep –

TWINKLEBERRY: Quite still –

MOSSTAIL: With his eyes closed –

TWINKLEBERRY: As if nothing had happened.
(*Pause.*
OLD BROWN towers over a recumbent NUTKIN, one huge claw around the squirrel's throat.)

MOSSTAIL: This looks like the end of the story.

TWINKLEBERRY: But it isn't.

MOSSTAIL: Old Brown carried Nutkin into his house.
(*OLD BROWN lugs NUTKIN in somehow. Hoots and squeaks.*)
He held him up by the tail, intending to skin him.

TWINKLEBERRY: But Nutkin pulled so very hard that his tail broke in two, and he dashed up the staircase and escaped out of the attic window.
(*NUTKIN, terrified, leaps from the tree, watched by SQUIRRELS and OLD BROWN. He limps to the front of the stage and shows what's left of his tail – not much.*)

MOSSTAIL: So there's not much left of the tail of Squirrel Nutkin.

TWINKLEBERRY: But if you meet Nutkin nowadays when he's up a tree and ask him a riddle –

NUTKIN: A riddle! I hate riddles!

TWINKLEBERRY: If you do ask him a riddle – he will throw sticks at you, and stamp his feet and scold, and shout –

NUTKIN: Cuck-cuck-cuck-cur-r-r-cuck-k-k!

OLD BROWN: Excuse me, young Nutkin, may I ask you a riddle?

NUTKIN: (*Cringing.*) A riddle, sir?

OLD BROWN: Tell me, Nutkin – when is a tail not a tail?
(*NUTKIN throws sticks, stamps his feet and scolds.*)

NUTKIN: Cuck-cuck-cuck-cur-r-r-cuck-k-k! Cuck-cuck-cuck-cur-r-r-cuck-k-k! (*Sings.*)
I'm a red squirrel
And I live in a tree
You'll never see a finer
Squirrel than me
I'm all red and furry
From my head to my toes
And I wave my tail
And I wrinkle my nose.

TWINKLEBERRY: (*Sings.*)
I'm a red squirrel
And I live in a tree
You'll never see a finer
Squirrel than me –

NUTKIN: (*Sings.*)
Except me!

NUTKIN & TWINKLEBERRY: (*Sing.*)
We're all red and furry
From our head to our toeses
And we wave our tails
And we wrinkle our noses.

SQUIRRELS: (*Sing.*)
Oh we're all red squirrels
And we live in a tree
You'll never see finer
Squirrels than we –

NUTKIN: (*Sings.*)
Except me!

SQUIRRELS: (*Sing.*)
> **We're all red and furry**
> **From our head to our toeses**
> **And we wave our tails**
> **And we wrinkle our noses**
> **And we wave our tails**
> **Goodbye!**

BEATRIX: But it's only goodbye for fifteen minutes. Because we're going to have an interval now so you can talk to each other and go to the lavatory and perhaps have a drink or a snack. But we'll see you after that for the Tale of Jeremy Fisher and the Tale of Samuel Whiskers.

(*Interval.*)

ACT TWO

Enter BEATRIX POTTER and ANIMALS, with umbrellas.

BEATRIX & ANIMALS: (*Sing.*)
>Dit dit dit dit
>Dit dit dit dit
>Rain rain
>Running down the lane
>Dit dit dit dit
>Dit dit dit dit
>Rain rain
>Who likes the rain?
>Roses like the rain
>Ducks like the rain
>And so does the mud in a bog, bog, bog!
>Daisies like the rain
>Fish like the rain
>And so does the friendly old frog, frog, frog!
>Dip dip dip dip
>Dip dip dip dip
>Rain rain
>Gurgling down the drain
>Drip drip drip drip
>Drip drip drip drip
>Rain rain
>Who likes the rain?
>Roses like the rain
>Ducks like the rain
>And so does the mud in a bog, bog, bog!
>Daisies like the rain
>Fish like the rain
>And so does the friendly old frog, frog, frog!
>
>(*Enter JEREMY FISHER, leaping up to BEATRIX POTTER.*)

JEREMY: Please Miss Potter, please tell my story. It's just
the story for a rainy day. For I am the friendliest old frog

33

in the world. (*He produces a little bouquet for her.*)
Kingcups. From my pond.

BEATRIX: Thank you Jeremy. They're beautifully golden.

JEREMY: Just like me! Just like me!

BEATRIX: No, Jeremy. You are beautifully green. Now I
will tell your story – The Tale of Mr Jeremy Fisher.
(*JEREMY poses proudly in the window of his watery house
reading a damp newspaper.*)
Once upon a time there was a frog called Mr Jeremy
Fisher. He lived in a little damp house amongst the
buttercups at the edge of a pond. The water was all
slippy-sloppy in the larder and in the kitchen.
(*JEREMY slops about carrying a jug and dishes.*)

JEREMY: (*Sings.*)

> **Slippy-sloppy, slippy-sloppy, that suits me.**
> **I like to get my feet all wet,**
> **There's nobody to scold.**
> **Slippy-sloppy, slippy-soppy, happy as can be.**
> **And I never ever catch a cold –**
> **Slippy-sloppy, slippy-sloppy –**

(*JEREMY notices Mrs SNAIL climbing up the wall.*)
Good morning, Mr Snail, how are you?

SNAIL: Taking it easy, Mr Jeremy Fisher. Taking it slowly.
How are you?

JEREMY: Happy and hoppy and – slippy-sloppy, Mrs
Snail! Now let's look out the window and see what we
can see. (*Opens a window.*) Whoopee! It's raining! Great
big drops splashing in the pond. (*Picks up a spade and a
round tin.*) Out we go, into the garden! (*Walks into his
garden, puts down the tin which is marked BAIT and proceeds
to dig.*) I will get some worms and go fishing and catch a
dish of minnows for my dinner. Minnows are my
favourite little fishes. (*Puts some worms in the tin.*) One
worm, two worms, three worms, four. If I catch more
than five fish, I will invite my friends round for dinner.
(*Digs again, puts more worms in the tin.*) Five worms, six
worms, seven worms, more! Yes, I will invite my friends
Mr Alderman Ptolemy Tortoise and Sir Isaac Newton.

The Alderman is a very important tortoise, but he eats only salad. Sir Isaac Newton is a very wise newt and he loves minnows. That's enough worms. Now I must get ready to go fishing. First I put on my macintosh. (*Pulls on a green mack.*) And a pair of shiny goloshes. (*Puts on goloshes.*) I take down my fishing rod. And my fish basket. I think that's everything. (*Checks.*) Macintosh. Goloshes. Fishing rod. Basket. Yes. And now off I hop to find my boat.

(*Sings.*)
Off I hop hop hop
To catch a bumper supper
And I'll never stop
Till I've caught myself a whopper
Yes I hop hop hop
I'm a flopper and a plopper
As I hop till I drop
For I'm a proper hopper
Yes I hop till I drop
For I'm a proper hopper.

Ah, here's my boat. As you see it's round and green – very like the other water-lily leaves. (*Stands on his boat and unties it from a water-plant's stem.*) I take a reed pole. (*Pulls a long reed like a bamboo pole out of the pond.*) Now I can push my boat out into open water. (*Confidentially.*) I know a good place for minnows. (*Punts his lily-pad boat along till he finds the place.*) I stick my pole into the mud, and fasten my boat to it. You see? Now. (*He settles himself down cross-legged.*) Where's my fishing tackle. (*Shows his float.*) You see, I have the dearest little red float. When it bobs up and down on the water, I know I've caught myself a fish. My fishing rod's a tough stalk of grass. My fishing line is a fine long white horse-hair from a fine old horse. I tie a little wriggling worm to the end of the line. Like this. Throw the line in the water. And then I wait. (*Sings.*)
I wait
And I wait

For a fish to take my bait
As I sit on my lily pad boat
I wait
As the rain
Trickles down my back
And I stare at my little red float
And wait
And wait
And wait.
Sometimes I doze and dream that I'm a tadpole
Caught in the beak of a terrible swan
I'm wriggling and squiggling but I can't get free
Then I wake with a start and the swan has gone –
And I wait
And I wait
Like a jelly on a plate
With the drops bouncing on to my nose
I wait
As the rain
Drizzles down the front
Of my not very waterproof clothes
And I wait
And wait
And wait
And wait –

About time for some lunch. Let's see what I put in my basket. Ah, good. A lovely butterfly sandwich. That's a good lunch to munch. (*Eats this small but remarkable sandwich very quickly.*) Hmmm! Good.

BEATRIX: But there was a great big water-beetle underneath the lily leaf.

(*BEETLE pops up and its claws pinch one of JEREMY's feet.*)

JEREMY: Hey, Mr Water-Beetle, don't tweak the toes of my goloshes. I didn't like that. I'd better cross my legs up shorter. (*Does so.*) Have another sandwich, Mr Jeremy Fisher. I think I will, thank you. (*Takes another and gobbles it.*)

BEATRIX: Once or twice something moved about with a rustle and a splash amongst the rushes at the side of the pond.

(*Splashing and rustling sounds.*)

JEREMY: I hope that's not a rat. I think I'd better get away from here.

(*JEREMY pushes his boat out a little way and drops in his line. Almost at once something tugs on the line.*)

Oh! My float! It gave a tremendous bobbit! I've caught something! I'm sure! Yes! A minnow! A minnow! I have him by the nose! (*Jerks up his rod – but on the line is a stickleback covered with spines.*) Oh no! You're not a smooth fat minnow! You're little Jack Sharp the Stickleback. And you're all covered with spiky spines.

(*JACK SHARP flounders about on the boat gasping.*)

JEREMY: Stop pricking me, Jack Sharp! Stop snapping at me!

JACK SHARP: (*Snapping and wriggling.*) Your fault, Mr Jeremy Fisher! You caught me, now I've caught you.

(*Takes a jump too far and lands in the water.*)

JEREMY: Back in the water, thank goodness. Off you go, Jack Sharp.

(*Heads of little fishes rise out of the water and laugh at JEREMY.*)

I do not like being laughed at by little fishes.

(*They laugh even harder, then vanish.*)

BEATRIX: While Mr Jeremy sat disconsolately on the edge of his boat – sucking his sore fingers and peering down into the water – a much worse thing happened. A really frightful thing it would have been, if Mr Jeremy had not been wearing his macintosh.

(*A huge TROUT rises up – ker-pflop-p-p-p! splash – and seizes JEREMY in its mouth.*)

BEATRIX: A great big enormous trout came up and it seized Mr Jeremy with a snap.

JEREMY: Ow! Ow! Ow!

BEATRIX: Then it turned and dived down to the bottom of the pond. (*Peers down into the pond.*) The trout wanted to eat Mr Jeremy Fisher for lunch. But it was so displeased with the taste of the macintosh, that in less than half a minute it spat him out again.

JEREMY: (*His head emerging from the water.*) That terrible trout!

BEATRIX: What happened, Jeremy?

JEREMY: (*Spluttering.*) It swallowed my fine goloshes.

BEATRIX: You were lucky to escape with your life. How did you get away?

JEREMY: I bounced up to the surface of the water like a cork. But I can't stop to chat. The trout may try another munch. (*Swims desperately to the shore.*)

BEATRIX: Jeremy swam with all his might to the edge of the pond. He scrambled out on the first bank he came to, and he hopped home across the meadow with his macintosh all in tatters.

JEREMY: (*Sings.*)

> **Off I flop flop flop**
> **Please don't eat me up for supper**
> **And I'll never stop**
> **Even if I come a cropper**
> **Yes I flop flop flop**
> **I'm a sorry whipper-snapper**
> **As I flop till I drop**
> **For I'm a proper flopper**
> **Yes I flop till I drop**
> **For I'm a proper flopper**

(*Staggering up to his house.*) What a mercy that fish was a trout and not an enormous pike! I've lost my rod and basket. But it doesn't much matter, for I'd never dare go fishing again!

BEATRIX: Jeremy put some sticking plaster on his fingers, and his friends both came to dinner. He could not offer them fish, but he had something else in his larder.

(*Enter Sir ISAAC NEWTON, a newt.*)

ISAAC: Good evening, Mr Jeremy Fisher.

JEREMY: You are welcome, Sir Isaac Newton. I do admire your black and gold waistcoat.

(Enter Mr ALDERMAN PTOLEMY TORTOISE, with a string bag.)

PTOLEMY: Good evening, Mr Jeremy Fisher.

JEREMY: You are welcome too, Mr Alderman Ptolemy Tortoise. I see you have brought your own salad.

PTOLEMY: Salad is the best food in the world.

ISAAC: But you like fish, don't you, Mr Jeremy?

JEREMY: Fish? I like fish? No, no, Sir Isaac, you must be thinking of somebody else.

PTOLEMY: That's odd, Mr Jeremy. I could have sworn you were very fond of fish.

ISAAC: Very fond of fish.

JEREMY: Never. To tell you the truth, my friends, I don't care if I never see a fish for the rest of my life. Come into dinner.

(JEREMY, PTOLEMY and ISAAC sit down at a table laid with a plate covered by a silver salver.)

PTOLEMY: What's for dinner, Jeremy?

ISAAC: Is it a nice dish of minnows?

JEREMY: Minnows? Never! *(He lifts the silver salver.)* There we are – a roasted grasshopper with lady-bird sauce.

(All three smile widely in anticipation.)

BEATRIX: Yes, for their dinner they had a roasted grasshopper with lady-bird sauce. Well, frogs consider that a beautiful treat. But I think it must have been nasty! Anyway, Mr Jeremy Fisher carved up that grasshopper and the three of them ate it all up. There's nothing more fun than a feast with your best friends. That's what I think. And the best way to finish a feast is with a good pudding – a good pud! And it's the best way to finish The Tale of Jeremy Fisher.

BEATRIX: Do you know what my favourite pudding is? My favourite is Roly-Poly Pudding. Here's how I make a Roly-Poly Pudding. *(Takes out a table with a pastry-board and equipment on it.)* I roll out my pastry into an oblong shape like this. *(Sings.)*

Rollaway thin
Rollaway thick

Rollaway thin and thickly
Rollaway slow
Rollaway quick
Rollaway slow and quickly
Rollaway quick
Rollaway slow
Rollaway quick and slowly
Spread jam from the pot
And what have you got?
You've got a roly-poly!

(*Rolls the pastry and shows it to audience, and spreads jam on it, all during the song.*)

But we can't eat it yet! I have to damp it round the edges like this. And roll it up like this. Then I put it in a baking tin. Spread on a tablespoon of butter. Then two cups of cold water. (*Popping the pudding in the oven.*) And bake in a hot oven for two or three hours. (*Taking a cooked and steaming pudding from the oven.*) And that's a jam roly-poly pudding! But now I want to tell you a story about another roly-poly pudding. But it wasn't a jam roly-poly. It was a kitten roly-poly! And this story, which is about cats and kittens and rats and a dog – is called The Tale of Samuel Whiskers or The Roly-Poly Pudding. Now once upon a time there was an old cat, called Mrs Tabitha Twitchit.

(*Enter TABITHA looking around her anxiously.*)

TABITHA: Have you seen my kittens, Miss Potter?

BEATRIX: Not one of them, Mrs Tabitha Twitchit.

TABITHA: I'm always losing them. Miss Moppet! Mittens! Tom Kitten!

(*MOPPET and MITTENS are watching her from hiding places.*)

BEATRIX: They must be a handful.

TABITHA: You mean a pawful. Yes, they're an awful pawful. Whenever they're lost they are always in mischief! Moppet! Mittens! Tom! It's baking day and I'm determined to shut them up in a cupboard so they won't steal my pastry.

(*MOPPET and MITTENS half-emerge from hiding places.*
TABITHA double-takes on them. Springs after them.)
TABITHA: (*Sings.*)
   Moppet and Mittens
   You naughty little kittens
   Come to me now
   Or I'll make you miaow!
MOPPET & MITTENS: (*Sing.*)
   We won't let you catch us mama!
   That's for sure.
   You'll shut us in the cupboard
   Like you did before!
   (*TABITHA, MOPPET and MITTENS sing their verses again,*
   now in counterpoint, as they run around the stage in an
   athletic chase.
   TABITHA catches MOPPET first, by the scruff of the neck.)
MOPPET: Put me down, mama, put me down!
   (*TABITHA pops MOPPET into the cupboard, shuts the door.*)
TABITHA: And now for Mittens.
   (*TABITHA catches MITTENS, who has stopped to watch*
   MOPPET's plight.)
MITTENS: Put me down, mama, put me down!
   (*TABITHA pops MITTENS into the cupboard, just manages*
   to keep MOPPET from breaking out before shutting the door.
   TABITHA leans against the door and sighs deeply.)
TABITHA: Now where's that Tom Kitten? I'll try the pantry
   under the staircase. (*Looks in there.*) No Tom Kitten! I'll
   try the best spare bedroom. (*Looks in there.*) No Tom
   Kitten! I'll go right to the top of the stairs and look in
   the attics. (*Round the stairs and looks in the attic.*) No Tom
   Kitten anywhere. There are so many hiding places you
   see, for it's an old, old house, full of cupboards and
   passages. Some of the walls are very thick, and there are
   odd little jagged doorways in them. And things disappear
   at night – especially cheese and bacon. Oh where can my
   Tom Kitten be?
   (*TABITHA mews sadly.*

> *But the cupboard door opens – out come MOPPET and*
> *MITTENS – they go straight to the stove where there is*
> *dough in a pan.)*

MITTENS: Look, Moppet, what's this stuff?

MOPPET: (*Patting dough with her paws.*) I don't know, but it's nice and soft.

MITTENS: (*Patting the dough.*) So it is. I think it's dough.

MOPPET: Muffins are made of dough.

MITTENS: Shall we make some muffins?

> (*A sudden knock at the door. MOPPET and MITTENS take*
> *fright and hide. Enter MRS RIBBY, a gingerish tabby cat in*
> *a bonnet, with a basket on her arm.*)

MRS RIBBY: Hello! Hello! Anybody home? It's only Mrs Ribby, come to see if I can borrow some yeast.

TABITHA: (*Comes downstairs mewing.*) Oh, come in Cousin Ribby, come in, and sit down! I'm in sad trouble, Cousin Ribby. (*Miaows and wipes away a tear.*) I've lost my dear son Thomas. I'm afraid the rats have got him.

MRS RIBBY: Tom Kitten is a bad kitten, Cousin Tabitha. He made a cat's cradle of my best bonnet last time I came to tea. Where have you looked for him?

TABITHA: All over the house! The rats are too many for me. What a thing it is to have an unruly family!

MRS RIBBY: I'm not afraid of rats. I will help you to find him, and punish him too!

TABITHA: Oh, dear me, Cousin Ribby – now Moppet and Mittens are gone! They have both got out of the cupboard! Where are those rascals?

MRS RIBBY: We must make a thorough search, Mrs Tabitha Twitchit.

> (*Door bangs, followed by scuttering sound.*)

I do believe that was somebody scuttering downstairs.

TABITHA: Rats, Cousin Ribby. Last Saturday I saw the old father rat – an enormous fellow. I was going to jump on him. But he showed his yellow teeth at me and whisked down a hole.

MRS RIBBY: Dear me, that sounds like that wicked rat, Mr Samuel Whiskers.

(*A rolling noise is heard from below.*)

Listen! I heard a curious roly-poly noise under the floor.

TABITHA: (*Peering between the floorboards.*) I can't see anything.

MRS RIBBY: (*Dragging MOPPET out of hiding.*) Here's one of your kittens at least.

TABITHA: (*Shaking MOPPET.*) Moppet, you scruffkitten.

MOPPET: Oh! Mother! Mother! There's been an old woman rat in the kitchen, and she's stolen some of the dough.

MRS RIBBY: That sounds like Anna Maria. She's married to Mr Samuel Whiskers.

TABITHA: (*Inspecting dough pan.*) Look! A lump of dough has gone.

MRS RIBBY: There are marks of little scratching fingers.

TABITHA: Which way did she go, Moppet?

MOPPET: I was too frightened to watch her.

TABITHA: Hold paws with me while we find Mittens and Tom.

(*TABITHA spots MITTENS and pulls her out of hiding.*)

TABITHA: Mittens! You saucy catlet!

MITTENS: Oh, Mother, Mother! There has been an old man rat in the dairy – a dreadful, 'normous big rat, mother; and he stole a pat of butter and the rolling-pin.

TABITHA: A rolling-pin and butter! Oh my poor son Thomas!

MRS RIBBY: A rolling-pin? Didn't we hear a roly-poly noise under the floor? Listen.

(*The sound of rolling from below.*)

Send for that friendly carpenter dog, John Joiner. Tell him to bring his saw.

BEATRIX: Now this is what had been happening to Tom Kitten, and it shows how very unwise it is to go up a chimney in a very old house, where a person does not know his way, and where there are enormous rats.

(*Enter TOM KITTEN.*)

TOM: I didn't want to be shut in a cupboard. I decided to hide in the chimney. (*Goes to the fire, begins to climb the chimney.*)

BEATRIX: The chimney was wide and there was plenty of room for a little Tom Cat.

(*TOM is prodding and exploring the chimney.*)

I wouldn't climb any further than that, myself, but Tom did. He took a big jump and landed on a ledge high up in the chimney, knocking down some of the soot.

(*Sootfall, coughing and choking overhead now TOM is up in the chimney and somewhat frightened.*)

TOM: I'd better climb right to the top. Then I can get out on the roof and try to catch sparrows. (*Climbing.*) It's very dark and sooty.

BEATRIX: Tom Kitten was getting very frightened! He climbed up, and up, and up.

TOM: (*Sings.*)

> Up I go, up I go,
> I've been climbing for an hour
> Though it's sooty and spooky
> And too dark to see
> Up I go, up I go,
> Up this smokey chokey tower
> But I'm a brave explorer
> And you can't scare me!

(*A noise. TOM jumps with fright.*)

What's that? I think I'm lost. What's this? Oh, someone's made a hole in the wall here. A bone! That's funny. Who's been gnawing bones in the chimney? I wish I'd never come!

(*Sings.*)

> Up I go, up I go,
> For I am lion-hearted
> But the chimney's so smelly
> And so slippery
> Up I go, up I go,
> Oh I wish I hadn't started!
> But I'm a brave explorer
> And you can't scare me!

(*Another noise. TOM jumps again.*)

What's that funny smell? Something like mouse; only
dreadfully strong. Atishoo! The smell made me sneeze. I
wonder if I can squeeze through this hole in the wall.

BEATRIX: Tom squeezed and squeezed till he got himself
through. But all at once he fell head over heels in the
dark, down a hole, and landed on some very dirty rags.
(*TOM tumbles on to a heap of rags. Dazed, he picks himself
up.*)

TOM: What's happened? Where am I?

BEATRIX: He was in a very small stuffy fusty room hung
with cobwebs. And sitting there was an enormous rat.
(*SAMUEL WHISKERS, a large rat in yellow white trousers
and a green jacket, sits on the floor looking at TOM.*)

SAMUEL: What do you mean by tumbling into my bed all
covered with smuts of soot?

TOM: (*Scared.*) Please sir, the chimney wants sweeping.

SAMUEL: Anna Maria! Anna Maria!
(*Pattering noise.*)

ANNA MARIA: Coming, Samuel!
(*Enter ANNA MARIA, a savage rat in a blue dress. She
looks at SAMUEL.*)
A dear little kitten, Mr Samuel Whiskers!

SAMUEL: Indeed, Anna Maria, a dear little kitten. Prepare
him!
(*ANNA MARIA leaps upon TOM, tears off his blue jacket
and ties him up with string.
SAMUEL observes and also inspects TOM's jacket.*)

SAMUEL: Tie him up tightly, Anna Maria. With very hard
knots if you please.

TOM: I want to go home. I want to go home!

ANNA MARIA: He's all tied up, Samuel.

SAMUEL: Anna Maria, Anna Maria – make me a kitten
dumpling roly-poly pudding for my dinner.

ANNA MARIA: I shall need dough and a pat of butter, and
a rolling-pin. (*She looks at TOM KITTEN with her head on
one side, considering him as a pudding.*)

SAMUEL: No. Make it properly, Anna Maria, with
breadcrumbs.

ANNA MARIA: Nonsense! Butter and dough.

SAMUEL: Very well, I'll just pop out through this hole in the wall.

ANNA MARIA: (*Sings.*)

Roly-poly pudding I sing
Tie up a kitten in lots of string
Roly-poly pudding I take
And pop in a very hot oven to bake
A helping for you and a helping for me
It's roly-poly pudding for tea!

SAMUEL: (*Emerging with butter, hands it over.*) Here's the butter, I'm off to get the rolling-pin. You'd better fetch some dough, Anna Maria. Oh, but what about the kitten?

ANNA MARIA: He'll never escape from my tight little knots. You find the rolling-pin, I'll bring the dough.
(*SAMUEL and ANNA MARIA scatter in different directions. SAMUEL finds the rolling pin and rolls it along the floor, past RIBBY and TABITHA, who do not notice him.*)

TABITHA: If Tom Kitten isn't back soon, he'll miss his tea.

MRS RIBBY: It's not like Thomas to miss tea-time.
(*ANNA MARIA finds the dough. She takes a small saucer and scoops up dough to put in it with her paws. She doesn't see that MOPPET is watching her.*)

BEATRIX: While Tom Kitten was left alone under the floor, he wriggled about and tried to mew for help. But his mouth was full of soot and cobwebs. He could not make anyone hear him.
(*A SPIDER puppet dangles down near TOM.*)
Except a spider, which came out of a crack in the ceiling and examined the knots critically, from a safe distance. It was a judge of knots because it had a habit of tying up unfortunate blue-bottles. It did not offer to help him.
(*Exit SPIDER puppet.*)
Tom Kitten wriggled and squirmed till he was quite exhausted.
(*SAMUEL and ANNA MARIA return.*)

SAMUEL: All right, let's make this kitten into a dumpling.

ANNA MARIA: Yes. First we smear him with butter.

SAMUEL and ANNA MARIA: (*Sing as they smear TOM.*)

> **Roly-poly pudding I sing**
> **Tie up a kitten in lots of string**
> **Roly-poly pudding I take**
> **And pop in a very hot oven to bake**
> **A helping for you and a helping for me**
> **It's roly-poly pudding for tea!**

ANNA MARIA: Now we roll him in the dough.

(*They do so, talking the while.*)

SAMUEL: Won't the string be very indigestible, Anna Maria?

ANNA MARIA: I don't think that matters much. But I wish this kitten would keep his head still. It spoils the pastry. I had better hold his ears.

(*She does so.*
TOM KITTEN is now in a sort of sausage of pastry, being rolled by the two rats with the rolling-pin.)

SAMUEL & ANNA MARIA (*Sing.*)

> **Roly-poly.**
> **Roly, roly,**
> **Poly, roly,**
> **Roly-poly for me!**

SAMUEL: His tail is sticking out! You didn't fetch enough dough, Anna Maria.

ANNA MARIA: I fetched as much as I could carry.

SAMUEL: It won't be a very good pudding. It smells sooty.

ANNA MARIA: Samuel! What's that?

(*From above there is a terrible rasping noise of a saw on wood and the noise of a little dog scratching and yelping.*)

SAMUEL: It's the sound of a carpenter's saw.

ANNA MARIA: And the sound of a dog!

SAMUEL: It must be that dog who's a carpenter – John Joiner!

(*A saw breaks a hole and the head of JOHN JOINER pushes through.*)

JOHN: Yes, it is me, John Joiner!

ANNA MARIA & SAMUEL: Dog! Dog! Dog!

(*ANNA MARIA and SAMUEL run away fast, whisking their tails behind them.*)

TOM: Rescue me, John Joiner!

JOHN: I'd rather chase those rats. But I'll rescue you, Tom.
(*He tears the string off TOM, who jumps up and pats him.*)
What a smell of rats! Hmmm!

TOM: How did you find me?

MOPPET: (*Suddenly appearing.*) I saw that Anna Maria at
her stealing. So I followed her and told John Joiner
where to look!

TOM: (*Embracing her.*) You're a hero, Miss Moppet!

BEATRIX: John Joiner nailed the plank down again, put his
tools in his bag and brought Tom Kitten downstairs. The
cat family had quite recovered. They invited John to stay
for a special dinner.

MOPPET: The dumpling was peeled off Tom Kitten. It was
made into a steamed pudding, with currants in it to hide
the sooty smuts.

TOM: I had to be put into a hot bath to get the butter off.

TWITCHIT: You will stay for dinner won't you, John
Joiner?

JOHN: I don't think I can –

TWITCHIT: Just smell this lovely bag pudding!

JOHN: (*Sniffs.*) Very nice, thank you. But I'd better not stay.
I've just finished making a wheelbarrow for Miss Potter,
and she's ordered two hen-coops.

BEATRIX: You know, when I was going to post a letter late
in the afternoon – I looked up the lane from the corner,
and I saw Mr Samuel Whiskers and his wife on the run,
with big bundles on a little wheelbarrow, which looked
very like mine.
(*SAMUEL WHISKERS and ANNA MARIA running.*
She pushes a wheelbarrow full of their belongings.)

SAMUEL: (*Puffing, out of breath.*) Are you sure this is the
way, Anna Maria?

ANNA MARIA: Certain sure, Samuel. Farmer Potatoes has
an old barn just through this gate. Much safer for us, I
think.
(*SAMUEL and ANNA MARIA exit.*)

BEATRIX: I am sure I never said Anna Maria could borrow
my wheelbarrow! I saw her and Samuel going into that

barn. After that, there were no more rats for a long time at Tabitha Twitchit's. Good morning, Farmer Potatoes! (*Enter FARMER POTATOES. He's a burly man with brown trousers and a greeen jacket, and a grey hat. He looks a bit like SAMUEL.*)

POTATOES: Miss Potter, they're driving me crazy. There are rats, and rats, and rats in my barn! They eat up the chicken food, and steal the oats and bran.

BEATRIX: I'm afraid they're the children and grand-children and great-grand-children of Mr and Mrs Samuel Whiskers!

POTATOES: There's no end to them!

BEATRIX: Why don't you have a word with Miss Moppet and Mittens? They have grown up into very good rat-catchers. Moppet! Mittens!

(*Enter MOPPET and MITTENS, followed by TOM Kitten.*)

POTATOES: Moppet! Mittens! Will you catch my rats for me?

MOPPET: Glad to, Farmer Potatoes.

MITTENS: After we catch them, we hang up the rats' tails on your barn door.

MOPPET: To show how many we've caught.

POTATOES: That's fair. And what about you, Tom Kitten? Can I count on you to go after my rats as well?

TOM: (*Scared silly.*) Rats? For a moment I thought you said rats, Farmer Potatoes. I'm afraid not. I have nothing to do with rats. But do call on me if you have any trouble with – er – mice. Small mice.

(*Enter as many of the ANIMALS from the four plays as possible.*)

BEATRIX: (*To audience.*) And that is the end of The Tale of Samuel Whiskers or The Roly-Poly Pudding. Thank you all for coming to see us. I hope you will read my stories and write lots of stories of your own. We'd like to say goodbye to you with one of our songs.*

---

* Or she could say 'with some of our songs', if there is time for a reprise of a few favourites.

BEATRIX & COMPANY: (*Sing.*)
> I had a cat and the cat pleased me
> I fed my cat by yonder tree;
> Cat goes fiddle-i-fee.
> I had a duck and the duck pleased me
> I fed my duck by yonder tree;
> Duck goes quack quack,
> Cat goes fiddle-i-fee.
> I had a squirrel and the squirrel pleased me
> I fed my squirrel by yonder tree;
> Squirrel goes chatter chatter,
> Duck goes quack quack,
> Cat goes fiddle-i-fee.
> I had a frog and the frog pleased me
> I fed my frog by yonder tree:
> Frog goes croaky croak, croaky croak
> Squirrel goes chatter chatter,
> Duck goes quack quack,
> Cat goes fiddle-i-fee.
> I had a dog and the dog pleased me
> I fed my dog by yonder tree;
> Dog goes bow-wow, bow-wow,
> Frog goes croaky croak, croaky croak,
> Squirrel goes chatter chatter,
> Duck goes quack quack,
> Cat goes fiddle-i-fee.

(*At the end of the song or songs, all the COMPANY wave goodbye to the audience.*)

Curtain.

Jemima Puddle-Duck and Her Friends

Songs

ACT ONE

1. I HAD A CAT – Beatrix Potter
2. PIT PAT PADDLE PAT – Jemima and Rebeccah
3. IT'S A WONDERFUL THING TO FLY – Jemima
4. WHICH LITTLE EGG – Fox and Jemima
5. PIT PAT PADDLE PAT (reprise) – Jemima and Ducklings
6. I HAD A CAT (reprise) – Beatrix Potter
7. RED SQUIRREL – Nutkin, Twinkleberry and Squirrels
8. ALL YOU LITTLE ANIMALS – Old Brown
9. IN AUTUMN TIME – Squirrels
10. RIDDLE ME – Nutkin
11. HITTY PITTY – Nutkin
12. A HOUSEFUL – Nutkin
13. PUDDING RIDDLE – Nutkin
14. HUM-A-BUM! BUZZ! – Nutkin
15. HICKAMORE HACKAMORE – Nutkin
16. RED SQUIRREL (reprise) – Squirrels

ACT TWO

1. WHO LIKES THE RAIN? – Beatrix Potter and Animals
2. SLIPPY SLOPPY – Jeremy Fisher
3. OFF I HOP– Jeremy Fisher
4. WAIT AND WAIT – Jeremy Fisher
5. OFF I FLOP – Jeremy Fisher
6. ROLLAWAY – Beatrix Potter
7. MOPPET AND MITTENS – Tabitha, Moppet and Mittens
8. UP I GO – Tom Kitten
9. ROLY-POLY PUDDING – Anna Maria and
   Samuel Whiskers
10. I HAD A CAT (reprise) – Beatrix Potter and Animals

PETER RABBIT
AND HIS FRIENDS

Characters

BEATRIX POTTER

BENJAMIN BUNNY

ROBIN REDBREAST

MR JACKSON
a toad

MRS THOMASINA TITTLEMOUSE
a wood mouse

GERTIE BEETLE

MRS MAISIE LADYBIRD

LOLA BUTTERFLY

IPSEY WIPSEY
a spider

BABBITY BUMBLE
a bee

BEES

PETER RABBIT

MRS RABBIT
Peter's mother

FLOPSY

MOPSY

COTTON-TAIL

MR McGREGOR
a gardener

SPIKKY SPARROW

OLD MOUSE

WHITE CAT

LUCIE
a little girl
TABBY KITTEN
SALLY HENNY-PENNY
COCK-ROBIN
MRS TIGGY-WINKLE

MRS McGREGOR
OLD MR BUNNY

Peter Rabbit and His Friends was first staged by the Unicorn Theatre for Children at the Pleasance Theatre on 8 February 2002. The company were:

MRS TITTLEMOUSE / MRS RABBIT / SALLY HENNY-PENNY, Abigail Bestwick

BENJAMIN BUNNY, Neil Gordon

LUCY / MR BUNNY, Lisa Milne Henderson

MRS TIGGY-WINKLE / WHITE CAT / BABBITY BUMBLE, Grethe Jensen

MR JACKSON / MR and MRS McGREGOR / TABBY KITTEN, Ian Jervis

BEATRIX POTTER, Georgina Sowerby

PETER RABBIT, Sophie Trott

Director Tony Graham

Composer and Music Director Stephen McNeff

Choreographer Emily Gray

Designer Russell Craig

Lighting Designer Jeanine Davies

ACT ONE

A garden in the country. Birdsong and quiet music. BEATRIX POTTER is sitting on a folding stool facing an easel. She has watercolours beside her and a jar of cloudy water to clean her brushes and she is studying the rabbit who crouches in front of her, his nose twitching. The rabbit is BENJAMIN BUNNY.

BENJAMIN: Miss Potter? (*He keeps painting.*) Miss Beatrix Potter?

BEATRIX: Yes, Benjamin Bunny.

BENJAMIN: What are you doing with that little tail on a stick?

BEATRIX: That's my paintbrush. I'm painting a picture.

BENJAMIN: And what are you painting a picture of?

BEATRIX: I'm painting you, Benjamin Bunny.

BENJAMIN: (*Pleased.*) Why do you like animals so much?
(*BEATRIX sings.*
As she sings, various ANIMALS appear, attracted by the music, and accompany her song with wordless singing. It's a bit like Orpheus singing and enchanting the wild animals.)

BEATRIX:
> When I was very small
> The town was very big
> My only friends were a wooden doll
> And a grimy little cotton pig.
> When I was very small
> Grown ups were enormous
> They never noticed me at all –
> A timid little dormouse.
> But whenever summertime came around
> We took a magical ride
> In a train that puffed all the way up to scotland
> And its windy, friendly-smelling countryside.
> Eagles and mountains
> And rocky little rivers
> The fox on the hill

And the frogs by the lake
Rabbits and hedgehogs
And tabby-cats and squirrels
They were my friends
And they danced for my sake.
Deer in the forest
And ducklings in the farmyard
The sheepdog who smiled
And the shy little snake
All of the creatures
The wild ones, the tame ones
They were my friends
And they sang for my sake.
I remember every stone
And the scent of the heather
And the growling of the thunder
And the shadows of the trees.
I remember the bats
As they flitted round the farmyard
And the strange deep music
Of the summer breeze.
Deer in the forest
And ducklings in the farmyard
The sheepdog who smiled
And the shy little snake
All of the creatures
The wild ones, the tame ones
They were my friends
And they sang for my sake.

Now Benjamin. Crouch down as you were before. And sit very still.

BENJAMIN Look everybody! Miss Beatrix Potter's painting me!

ROBIN REDBREAST: Paint me too, Miss Potter, please!

MR JACKSON: (*A large toad.*) Tiddly, widdly, Miss Potter. Paint me. There's much more to paint in a toad than a Robin Redbreast.

BEATRIX: (*Putting down her brush.*) Everybody, come and
look at Benjamin.
(*She holds up the painting and the ANIMALS smile and
applaud, especially BENJAMIN.*
*But PETER RABBIT is not impressed. PETER is bouncy,
full of energy, adventure-loving and so sometimes naughty –
but always endearing.*)

PETER: Do me now, Miss Potter.

BEATRIX: All animals who want to be painted – get into a
line.

PETER: Paint me first, please!

BEATRIX: Why you first, Peter Rabbit?

PETER: Because I'm the most important, I'm the most
famous.

ROBIN REDBREAST: Only because Miss Potter made a
book about you. Beatrix Potter is more famous than you.

BEATRIX: You must wait your turn, Peter. First I would
like to paint Mrs Tittlemouse.
(*Fetching MRS TITTLEMOUSE from the end of the line.*)

PETER: But what'll we do while you're painting her?

BEATRIX: I'll tell you a story.

PETER: Yes, tell my story.

BEATRIX: While I'm painting Mrs Tittlemouse, I'll tell her
story.

PETER: Why should a little wood-mouse go first?

BEATRIX: Because she's the humblest of all the animals. I
found her right at the end of the line.

MRS TITTLEMOUSE: But I don't have a story, Miss
Potter – I just try to keep my house nice and tidy.

BEATRIX: And that's a story in itself. So here is The Tale
of Mrs Tittlemouse. Once upon a time there was a wood-
mouse, and her name was Mrs Thomasina Tittlemouse.
(*MRS TITTLEMOUSE, a small mouse with a long tail,
appears in her doorway, hands clasped in front of her apron.
She nods to BEATRIX.*)
She lived in a grassy bank under a hedge. Such a funny
house!

BEATRIX: (*Sings.*)

I've heard that Mrs Tittlemouse
Lived in a tiny little house,
Thatched with a roof of rushes brown
And lined with hay and thistledown.

COMPANY: (*Sing.*)

Now wasn't that a lovely house
For Thomasina Tittlemouse?

BEATRIX: (*Sings.*)

This house had walls of grass and moss
Pegged down with willow twigs across.
Now wasn't that a lovely house
For Thomasina Tittlemouse?

COMPANY: (*Sing.*)

Now wasn't that a lovely house
For Thomasina Tittlemouse?

MRS TITTLEMOUSE: It's a fine house. It suits me. I have
yards and yards of sandy passages, all amongst the roots
of the hedge. It's all very neatly arranged. I fill up my
seed-cellars in summer and my nut-cellars in autumn. I
have a kitchen and a parlour and a pantry and a larder.
And there is my bedroom, where I sleep in a little box
bed. I'm a very tidy and particular mouse. You'll always
find me sweeping and dusting my softy sandy floors.
(*Sweeping with dustpan and brush.*) Who's that? Not Gertie
Beetle!

(*GERTIE BEETLE wanders in and leans against the wall.*)

GERTIE: 'Scuse me, Mrs Tittlemouse, it's these sandy
passages. They all look alike to me. I'm a bit lost.

MRS TITTLEMOUSE: (*Clattering her dust-pan.*) Lost,
stolen or strayed, Gertie, you shouldn't be in my house.
And you didn't wipe a single one of your six grubby
feet.

GERTIE: The hole I crawled in by didn't have a doormat.

MRS TITTLEMOUSE: If it didn't have a doormat, it
wasn't a door.

GERTIE: Sorry, Mrs Tittlemouse – I'm not good at
thinking.

MRS TITTLEMOUSE: No, but you're very good at creeping in where you're not wanted. Gertie, Gertie, you're so dirty! Shoo!
(*Off scuttles GERTIE.*
MRS TITTLEMOUSE sweeps, humming to herself.
MAISIE LADYBIRD approaches from the other direction.
She stops and looks at MRS TITTLEMOUSE cheekily.)
MAISIE: How delightful to see you, Mrs Tittlemouse!
MRS TITTLEMOUSE: That's as maybe, Mrs Maisie Ladybird. But I'm trying to clean my sandy floors.
MAISIE: I'm sure I'm not stopping you, Mrs Tittlemouse.
MRS TITTLEMOUSE: Oh, but I think you are.
MAISIE: It's about time for elevenses. You don't have a little something for me, do you?
MRS TITTLEMOUSE: Yes, I do. I have a song for you.
(*Sings.*)
> **Ladybird, ladybird,**
> **Fly away home,**
> **Your house is on fire**
> **And your children are gone;**
> **All except one**
> **And that's little Ann**
> **And she has crept under**
> **The frying pan.**
> **So ladybird, ladybird,**
> **Fly away home,**
> **Your house is on fire**
> **And your children are gone.**

I'm a very busy mouse, Mrs Ladybird – so off you go.
(*MAISIE spreads her wings and flies off.*
MRS TITTLEMOUSE turns to the audience.)
MRS TITTLEMOUSE: You see what I have to put up with! Grubby old beetles, chattersome ladybirds –
IPSEY: (*Appearing beside her.*) And big fat spiders!
MRS TITTLEMOUSE: What are you doing here, Ipsey Wipsey?
IPSEY: Beg pardon, is this not Miss Muffet's?
MRS TITTLEMOUSE: Do I look like Miss Muffet?

IPSEY: No, more like a tuffet. I just dropped in to shelter from the rain. You know the story – (*Sings.*)

Ipsey Wipsey Spider
Climbing up the spout;
Down came the rain
And washed the spider out.
Out came the sun and
Dried up all the rain –
Ipsey Wipsey Spider
Climbing up again.

MRS TITTLEMOUSE: (*Sings.*)

Ipsey Wipsey Spider
Go out in the rain.
Wait for the sun and
Climb your spout again.
I'm sweeping up and
I will sweep you out –
Ipsy Wipsey Spider
Go and climb your spout.

Away with you, you bold bad spider! Leaving ends of cobweb all over my nice clean house! Out of the window you must go. (*Bundling IPSEY out.*) You can let yourself down with a string.

(*Exit IPSEY, crestfallen.*)

That's better. (*Hangs up her dustpan and brush, wipes her paws on her apron and takes down a wicker basket with a handle.*) Now I'm off to my store-room to fetch some cherry-stones and thistle-down seed for dinner. (*She walks along, sniffing at the floor as she goes.*) Oh, I smell a smell of honey. Could it be the cowslips outside, in the hedge? I am sure I can see the marks of little dirty feet. (*She rounds a corner and is face to face with the large bee, BABBITY BUMBLE.*)

BABBITY: Zizz, Bizz, Bizz!

MRS TITTLEMOUSE: (*Aside.*) I wish I'd brought my broom. (*To BABBITY.*) Good-day Babbity Bumble. I'd like to buy some beeswax from you.

BABBITY: Zizz, Bizz, Bizz!

MRS TITTLEMOUSE: But what are you doing down here? Why do you always burst in at windows saying Zizz, Bizz, Bizz!

BABBITY: (*Peevishly.*) Zizz, Bizz, Bizz!

(*BABBITY, followed by MRS TITTLEMOUSE using her basket as a shield, goes to a storehouse door and opens it. It is apparently full of dry moss, into which BABBITY disappears.*)

MRS TITTLEMOUSE: That's the room where I keep my acorns. I ate them all before Christmas. So that storeroom should be empty. But it's full of scruffy dry moss.

(*MRS TITTLEMOUSE begins to pull out the moss. Three or four other BEES put their heads out and buzz fiercely.*)

BEES: Buzz! Buzz! Buzz!

MRS TITTLEMOUSE: That moss is full of bad-tempered bees. (*Raises her voice.*) I am not in the habit of letting lodgings; this is an intrusion! I'll have you turned out.

BEES: Buzz! Buzz! Buzz!

MRS TITTLEMOUSE: Who can help me?

BEES: Bizz! Wizz! Wizz!

MRS TITTLEMOUSE: Not Mr Jackson the toad. He never wipes his feet. I think I'll leave the bees till after dinner. Back to my parlour! I'll sit in my rocking chair and have a think.

BEES: Zizz! Bizz! Bizz! Zuzz! Buzz! Buzz!

(*MRS TITTLEMOUSE hurries back to her parlour Mr JACKSON, a very large toad, sits in MRS TITTLE-MOUSE's little rocking-chair, twiddling his thumbs and smiling, with his feet on the fender of the fireplace. He coughs in a fat voice.*)

MRS TITTLEMOUSE: How do you do, Mr Jackson? Deary me, you are wet.

JACKSON: Rainy times, Mrs Tittlemouse, rainy times. You'd notice these things if you lived in a drain, like me.

MRS TITTLEMOUSE: A drain in a very dirty wet ditch. You must be wetter than wetness, Mr Jackson.

JACKSON: Thank you, thank you, thank you, Mrs Tittlemouse! I'll sit awhile and dry myself at your fire.

MRS TITTLEMOUSE: Your coat does appear to be
dripping somewhat, Mr Jackson.
(*MRS TITTLEMOUSE takes a mop and wipes around MR
JACKSON, who coughs.*)
MRS TITTLEMOUSE: Perhaps you would like to take
some dinner?
JACKSON: (*Leaping to the table and sitting down expectantly.*)
Much obliged, Mrs Tittlemouse, much obliged.
MRS TITTLEMOUSE: (*Presenting a plate of three or four
cherrystones the size of small melons.*) Cherrystones, Mr
Jackson?
JACKSON: Thank you, thank you, Mrs Tittlemouse! No
teeth, no teeth, no teeth!
(*He opens his mouth most unnecessarily wide to demonstrate.*)
MRS TITTLEMOUSE: Perhaps a nice plate of thistledown
seed? (*Putting down the plate.*)
JACKSON: Tiddly, widdly, widdly!
Pouff, pouff, puff!
(*He blows the thistledown all over the room.*)
Thank you, thank you, thank you, Mrs Tittlemouse!
Now what I really – really should like – would be a little
dish of honey!
MRS TITTLEMOUSE: I am afraid I have not got any, Mr
Jackson.
JACKSON: Tiddly, widdly, widdly, Mrs Tittlemouse! I can
smell it; that is why I came to call.
(*JACKSON stands up from the table and begins to search
around in cupboards etc.*
*MRS TITTLEMOUSE follows him round with a mop wiping
his big footmarks off the parlour floor.*)
JACKSON: Tiddly, widdly, widdly! No honey in the
cupboards! No honey, Mrs Tittlemouse?
MRS TITTLEMOUSE: You will get stuck in the doorway,
Mr Jackson.
JACKSON: Tiddly, widdly, widdly, Mrs Tittlemouse! There
are three creepy-crawly woodlice hiding in this plate-
rack! Missed him! Missed him! Got him! (*He draws in his
tongue and swallows down a woodlouse.*) Very tasty. Now

let's see what's in the larder. (*Squeezing in.*) Good day,
Lola Butterfly – tasting the sugar, are you?

MRS TITTLEMOUSE: She's off and out of the window.

JACKSON: Tiddly, widdly, widdly, Mrs Tittlemouse; you
seem to have plenty of visitors!

MRS TITTLEMOUSE: All without invitations, Mr
Jackson!

(*MRS TITTLEMOUSE follows JACKSON along a passage,
where he nearly bumps into BABBITY.*)

BABBITY: Buzz! Wizz! Wizz!

JACKSON: Tiddly, widdly!

(*JACKSON snaps at BABBITY, then retreats, wiping his
mouth with his coat-sleeve.*)

JACKSON: I do not like bumble bees. They are all over
bristles.

BABBITY: Get out, you nasty old toad!

MRS TITTLEMOUSE: I shall go distracted! Miss Potter!
Miss Beatrix Potter!

BEATRIX: What's all the pother, Mrs Tittlemouse?

MRS TITTLEMOUSE: It's these visitors, Miss Potter. Well,
I can deal with the insects and spiders too. But Mr
Jackson is much too much for me – he's twice my size.

BEATRIX: Better hide yourself in your little box bed, Mrs
Tittlemouse. I'll tell you when it's safe to come out.

(*MRS TITTLEMOUSE hides behind the curtain of her box
bed.*
Mr JACKSON attacks the moss.)

JACKSON: There's a bee's nest in this moss. Where there's
bees there's honey. And where there's honey – there's Mr
Jackson. Tiddly, widdly!

BEES: (*Sing.*)

> **Zizz! Bizz! Zizz!**
> **Zuzz! Buzz! Buzz!**
> **We're going to sting you**
> **Till you explode!**
> **You batty old**
> **Ratty old**
> **Fatty old toad!**

Zizz! Bizz! Zizz!
Zuzz! Buzz! Buzz!
JACKSON: (*Sings.*)
   Tiddly, widdly, widdly!
   Slurp! Slorrup! Slurp!
   I love honey when it's runny
   Tiddly, widdly, burp!
   Out of my way, you buzzy little things
   'Cos I'm not afraid of your silly little stings
   Tiddly, widdly, widdly!
   Slurp! Slorrup! Slurp!
   (*The battle ends as MR JACKSON exits, triumphantly, with
   a great golden honeycomb.*)
BEATRIX: Thomasina Tittlemouse! (*A squeak.*) You can
   come out now.
MRS TITTLEMOUSE: (*Peeps out, hops out of bed and looks
   around.*) It's something dreadful! Never did I see such a
   mess – smears of honey. And lumps of moss!
   Thistledown everywhere. And marks of big and little
   dirty feet – all over my nice clean house! (*Tidying up all
   the time.*)
BEATRIX: What are you doing now, Mrs Tittlemouse?
MRS TITTLEMOUSE: Altering my front door, Miss
   Potter. I'll make it too small for Mr Jackson!
BEATRIX: Next morning Mrs Tittlemouse got up very
   early and began a spring cleaning which lasted a
   fortnight. She swept, and scrubbed, and dusted; and she
   rubbed up the furniture with beeswax, and polished her
   little tin spoons. When it was all beautifully neat and
   clean, she gave a party for some of her smaller friends,
   but not Mr Jackson.
   (*FRIENDS of MRS TITTLEMOUSE arrive and dance
   together.*)
   Mr Jackson smelt the party and came up the bank, but he
   could not squeeze in at the door.
   (*Mr JACKSON's face appears at the window watching the
   party.*)

MRS TITTLEMOUSE: Here Mr Jackson, have an acorn cup full of honey-dew. (*She passes one out to him.*) I'm sorry there's not room for you inside.

JACKSON: I'm not offended in the least, Mrs Tittlemouse. I like to sit out here in the sun. Tiddly, widdly, widdly! Your very good health, Thomasina Tittlemouse!

COMPANY: (*Sing and dance.*)

> **If acorn-cups were tea-cups**
> **What should we have to drink?**
> **Why honey-dew for sugar,**
> **In a cuckoo-pint of milk.**
> **Nid, nid, noddy, we stand in a ring**
> **All day long, and never do a thing!**
> **But nid, nid, noddy! We wake up at night,**
> **We hop and we dance in the merry moonlight!**
> **Laid out upon a toadstool**
> **On a cloth of cobweb silk**
> **With pats of witches' butter**
> **And a tansey cake I think!**
> **Nid, nid, noddy, we stand in a ring**
> **All day long, and never do a thing!**
> **But nid, nid, noddy! We wake up at night,**
> **We hop and we dance in the merry moonlight!**

BEATRIX: And that is the end of the Tale of Mrs Tittlemouse.

PETER: (*Leaping in front of BEATRIX.*) Here I am! Is it my turn?

BEATRIX: Peter Rabbit, I can't resist you.

PETER: Huzzah! Tell all the world sitting out there all about ME!

BEATRIX: I'm going to paint you while I tell your tale. So please sit still.

ANIMALS: (*Sing.*)

> **Sit still! Sit still!**

PETER: (*Sings.*)

> **I can't sit still**
> **I can't sit still**
> **I'm bursting at the seams**

>With schemes and dreams
>And I can't sit still

ANIMALS: (*Sing.*)

>Sit still! Sit still!

PETER: (*Sings.*)

>It's really frightening
>But a wonderful thrill
>My tummy's full of lightning
>And I can't sit still
>My heartbeat's doubling
>And my brains are bubbling
>Like Jack and Jill
>At the top of the hill
>I'm so excited
>I can't sit still!

BEATRIX, PETER & ANIMALS: (*Sing.*)

>Like Jack and Jill
>At the top of the hill
>He's/I'm so excited
>That he/I can't sit still!

BEATRIX: Here comes Peter's mother.

>(*MRS RABBIT bustles on.*)

>Old Mrs Rabbit is a widow –

MRS RABBIT: Yes, I lost my husband, it's a very sad story –

BEATRIX: So how do you earn your living, Mrs Rabbit?

MRS RABBIT: By knitting rabbit-wool mittens, Miss Potter.

BEATRIX: Yes, I once bought a pair at a bazaar.

MRS RABBIT: I also sell herbs, and rosemary tea, and rabbit-tobacco –

BEATRIX: That's what we call lavender.

PETER: (*Popping his head out, impatiently.*) That's enough about mittens and herbs. What about my story?

BEATRIX: Don't be so impatient, Peter Rabbit.

PETER: (*Popping down.*) Well, it's such a good story.

BEATRIX Then let's begin it. Once upon a time there were four little Rabbits, and their names were – Flopsy, Mopsy, Cotton-tail and Peter.

MRS RABBIT: (*Sings.*)
> **Once upon a time**
> **There were four little rabbits –**
> **Flopsy,**
> **Mopsy,**
> **Cotton-tail**
> **And Peter.**
> **They lived with their mother in a sand-bank**
> **Underneath the roots of a big fir-tree –**
> **Flopsy,**
> **Mopsy,**
> **Cotton-tail**
> **And Peter.**

BEATRIX: Well, let's meet them, Mrs Rabbit.

MRS RABBIT & BEATRIX: (*Sing.*)
> **Flopsy!**
> **Mopsy!**
> **Cotton-tail!**
> **And Peter!**

(*Nobody appears.*)

BEATRIX: No sign of them.

MRS RABBIT: Perhaps they can't hear us, way down in our rabbit hole home.

BEATRIX: (*To audience.*) Will you help us call them?

AUDIENCE: Yes!

BEATRIX, MRS RABBIT & AUDIENCE (Sing.)
> **Flopsy!**
> **Mopsy!**
> **Cotton-tail!**
> **And Peter!**

(*Still nothing.*)

BEATRIX: We'd better sing louder. Come on!

BEATRIX, MRS RABBIT & AUDIENCE: (*Sing.*)
> **Flopsy!**
> (*FLOPSY appears and nods to audience.*)
> **Mopsy!**
> (*MOPSY appears and nods.*)
> **Cotton-tail!**

(*COTTON-TAIL appears and nods, back to audience so the famous tail can be seen.*)
And Peter!
(*Nobody appears.*)
BEATRIX: Once more!
BEATRIX, MRS RABBIT & AUDIENCE: (*Sing.*)
Flopsy!
Mopsy!
Cotton-tail!
And Peter!
PETER: (*Appearing behind BEATRIX, MRS RABBIT and the rest, hands in the pockets of his famous blue jacket.*)
Boo!
(*BEATRIX, MRS RABBIT, FLOPSY, MOPSY and COTTON-TAIL jump.*)
PETER: It's all right. Don't worry. It's me! I'm here!
BEATRIX: And now at last we can begin – The Tale of Peter Rabbit!
PETER: Huzzah!
(*MRS RABBIT organizes her children. FLOPSY, MOPSY and COTTON-TAIL don red cloaks and take baskets. PETER doesn't listen.*)
MRS RABBIT: Now, my dears. You may go into the fields or down the lane, but don't go into Mr McGregor's garden. What did I say?
FLOPSY, MOPSY & COTTON-TAIL: You may go into the fields or down the lane, but don't go into Mr McGregor's garden.
PETER: Why not, Mama? It's an interesting-looking garden.
MRS RABBIT: Your father had an accident there. He was put in a pie by Mrs McGregor.
FLOPSY, MOPSY & COTTON-TAIL: Put in a pie?
MRS RABBIT: Yes, put in a pie. Now run along, and don't get into mischief. (*Taking a basket and an umbrella.*) I am going out.
FLOPSY: Where are you going, Mama?
MRS RABBIT: Down through the wood to the baker's shop. I shall buy a loaf of brown bread and five currant buns.

PETER: Five currant buns for me?

MRS RABBIT: One currant bun each.

FLOPSY, MOPSY & COTTON-TAIL: Huzzah!

(*Off walks MRS RABBIT to the wood.*)

BEATRIX: Flopsy, Mopsy and Cotton-tail were good little rabbits, so they went down the lane.

MOPSY: Look! In that hedge. Big bright blackberries.

(*MOPSY reaches up with a little walking stick to pull down blackberry branches.*

COTTON-TAIL picks the blackberries.

FLOPSY collects the fruit in the baskets. This begins in an orderly fashion, but during the song which follows the three rabbits perform more and more acrobatic feats to try to reach the berries at the top of the bramble bush, climbing on each other's shoulders etc, and the song ends in collapse in a heap.)

FLOPSY, MOPSY & COTTON-TAIL: (*Sing.*)

> The green little, mean little, lean little berries
> Are always at the bottom of the blackberry bush.
> But the biggest best berries are always high
> On the branches way up in the sky.
> Though the brambles may scratch
> We jump and we hop
> For we have to snatch
> The ones at the top
> Yes the green little, mean little, lean little berries
> Are always at the bottom of the blackberry bush.
> But the biggest best berries are always high
> On the branches way up in the autumn sky.
> And those berries we'll cart
> Back home to our mam
> For blackberry tart
> And blackberry jam
> For the biggest best berries are always high
> On the branches way up in the autumn sky
> For blackberry tarts!
> And blackberry jelly!
> And blackberry jam!
> And wonderful blackberry pie!

(*The three rabbits collapse in a heap.*)

BEATRIX: What good little rabbits. But Peter, who was very naughty, ran straight away to Mr McGregor's garden and squeeeeezed under the gate!
(*PETER races towards the garden and manages to squeeze under the gate.*)

PETER: (*Gazing around in wonder.*) Mr McGregor's garden. What a wonderful place!

PETER: (*Picking and eating – sings.*)
Let us have a lettuce,
Munch, munch, munch.
Next I'll chew a carrot,
Crunch, crunch, crunch.
Then I'll have a radish,
To finish my lunch.
For I'm sure that Mr McGregor's not here today.
Yes I'm sure that Mr McGregor has gone away
So –
Let us have a lettuce,
Munch, munch, munch.
Next I'll chew a carrot,
Crunch, crunch, crunch.
Then I'll have a radish,
To finish my lunch.

PETER: (*Feels his stomach.*)
Oh dear. Perhaps I ate my lunch too quick.
I'm feeling just a little – sick.
Mama says eating parsley
Helps when you're feeling gharsley.
No parsley here, no parsley there,
Can't see no parsley anywhere – ah!
(*PETER has come face to face with the ogre gardener, MR McGREGOR – planting out young cabbages with a dibber on his hands and knees.*
MR McGREGOR has spectacles, a red nose, a bushy white beard and a deerstalker hat.
To PETER he is frightening but he should also be a comic figure for children.)

MR McGREGOR: Who are you?

PETER: I'm Peter Rabbit. Who are you?

MR McGREGOR: I'm Mr McGregor – and I haven't gone
away.

PETER: Oh!

MR McGREGOR: I believe you like lettuces, and beans
and radishes?

PETER: I do. Do you like animals, sir?

MR McGREGOR: Oh yes, I'm a great aminal lover. (*Sings.*)

> **I loves all the aminals**
> **Crunchers great and small**
> **Birds and fish and beasties**
> **I do love 'em all**
> **I loves a chicken**
> **Strutting round the farm**
> **I walks beside her**
> **To keep her safe from harm**
> **I makes her cosy**
> **In her chicken coop**
> **You know how I likes her best?**
> **Chicken soup!**

MR MCGREGOR & PETER:

> **Clucka cluck cluck cluck cluck little chicken**
> **Clucka cluck cluck cluck cluck**

MR McGREGOR:

> **I loves a piggy**
> **Sitting in his sty**
> **I loves a piggy**
> **Shall I tell you why?**
> **I takes my piggy**
> **For a friendly stroll**
> **You know how I likes him best?**
> **Sausage roll!**

MR MCGREGOR & PETER:

> **Honka honk honk honk honk little piggy**
> **Honka honk honk honk honk**

MR McGREGOR:

> **I loves all the aminals**
> **Crunchers great and small**
> **Birds and fish and beasties**
> **I do love 'em all**

    I loves a fishy
    Swimming in a brook
    I reads my fishy
    A fishy story book
    I see me fishy
    And I licks me lips
    You know how I likes him best?
    Vinegar and chips!

MR MCGREGOR & PETER:
    Bubble bubble bubble bubble bub little fishy
    Bubble bubble bubble bub bub

MR McGREGOR: (*Advancing.*)
    I loves a bunny
    Likes to watch him jump
    Feeds him on carrots
    Till he's nice and plump
    Dear little bunny
    Apple of me eye
    You know how I likes him best?
    Rabbit pie!

(*MR McGREGOR pounces, but misses PETER. This is a cue for an almighty chase as MR McGREGOR runs after PETER, waving a rake – all around the garden, the stage and auditorium, with PETER trying to hide under seats etc. Musical mayhem. Chase should be planned to avoid scaring the small children.*)

MR McGREGOR: Stop thief! Have you seen a leetle rabbit? Stop thief!

BEATRIX: (*Like a racing commentator.*) Now it's Peter Rabbit, looking dreadfully frightened, just in the lead, with Mr McGregor on his tail. Peter rushing all over the garden, it looks as if he's forgotten the way back to the gate. Oh! Now he's lost one shoe among the cabbages. And there goes his other shoe amongst the potatoes! Now he's down on four legs, faster and faster – I think he's going to get away altogether, the Scottish gardener's lost sight of him, Peter's going to escape – oh no! – he's run into a gooseberry net, and he's caught by the big brass buttons on his new jacket!

(*PETER is twisted up in the gooseberry net and he can't get free.*

MR MCGREGOR is searching the garden for him, advancing towards PETER.)

PETER: (*Sobbing.*) I don't want to be put in a pie.

(*A friendly SPARROW flutters up.*)

SPARROW: Come on, mate! Move your tail!

PETER: I'm stuck, Spikky Sparrow!

SPARROW: You're not stuck. It's just your jacket what's stuck. Wriggle out of it and run for it.

PETER: (*Wriggling out of his jacket.*) Like this?

SPARROW: Move!

(*Only just in time. Mr McGREGOR has been stalking PETER with a sieve.*)

MR McGREGOR: I'll catch him in my trusty sieve. I'll pop it upon the top of Peter.

(*But PETER's away.*

The SPARROW flies alongside him.)

SPARROW: Well done, Peter. Now hide yourself, quick! Into that toolshed.

(*In the toolshed PETER spots a big green watering can.*)

PETER: Here's a good hiding place!

(*PETER jumps into the can.*

Splashing sounds.)

SPARROW: Well it would've been – if it hadn't got so much water in it. Good luck, mate!

(*SPARROW flies off.*)

MR McGREGOR: (*Stalking PETER.*) He must be round here somewhere. Under a flowerpot mebbe? (*Picking up flowerpots one by one, and looking carefully under each one.*) No rabbit. No rabbit.

PETER: (*Sneezing.*) Kertyschoo!

BEATRIX: And Mr McGregor is after him again and tries to put his foot upon Peter but the rabbit jumps out of a window, upsetting three plants. Oh yes, the window's too small for Mr McGregor, and he gives up! And he goes back to work.

(*PETER sits outside, panting.*)

PETER: It's no good. I don't know how to get out of this garden. And I'm very damp with sitting in that watering can.

BEATRIX: And off he wanders, going lippity-lippity, not very fast, looking all around. And he's found a door in a wall.

PETER: It's locked.

BEATRIX: And there's no room for a fat little rabbit to squeeze underneath.

(*An OLD MOUSE stops and stares at him, chewing a huge pea.*)

PETER: (*To OLD MOUSE.*) Do you know the way to the garden gate, madam Mouse?

OLD MOUSE: (*Still chewing.*) Sogglitty mug noggle. (*Swallows.*) Sorry – mouth full. I never saw the garden gate. I always nip out through this little gap when I'm carrying peas and beans to my family in the woods. So sorry.

(*Exit OLD MOUSE.*)

PETER: I'll try this path. That's a pretty pond. Oh.

(*A WHITE CAT sits beside a pond of water-lilies and goldfish, which may well be a cloth painting sloped so we can see it.*)

WHITE CAT: (*Sings.*)

White cat
White cat beside a pond
White cat sitting very still
White cat
White cat staring at the goldfish in the pond
White cat sitting very still
And just now and then
The tip of her tail
Twitches as if it were alive
White cat
White cat beside a pond
White cat sitting very still

PETER: I think it best to go away without speaking to her. I have heard about cats from my cousin, little Benjamin Bunny. Listen. I can hear the noise of Mr McGregor's hoe – scr-r-ritch, scratch, scratch, scritch. There he is –

hoeing onions. But he's not looking this way. And there's the gate!

BEATRIX: Peter starts running, fast as he can go, along the path behind the black-currant bushes. Mr McGregor spots him at the corner, but Peter keeps on, he slips under the gate and he's outside the garden, into the wood and safe at last!

MR McGREGOR: (*Suiting the action to the words.*) I think I'll hang up this little jacket for a scarecrow to frighten the blackbirds.

(*He chuckles to himself as he hangs up PETER's jacket.
MRS RABBIT is busily cooking as PETER rushes in, flops down on the floor and shuts his eyes.*)

MRS RABBIT: What have you done with your clothes, Peter Rabbit? That's the second little jacket and shoes that you've lost in a fortnight!

BEATRIX: I am sorry to say that Peter was not very well during the evening.

MRS RABBIT: Into bed you pop, Peter. Here's some camomile tea. Come on, you must take a dose – one table-spoonful to be taken at bed-time!

PETER: (*Drinking it against his will.*) Arrrgh! (*Turns over and pretends to sleep.*)

MRS RABBIT: Now, Flopsy, Mopsy and Cotton-tail. What would you like for your supper?

FLOPSY: We'd like bread, please mother.

MOPSY: And milk, please mother.

FLOPSY, MOPSY & COTTON-TAIL: (*Sing.*)
   And blackberry tarts!
   And blackberry jelly!
   And blackberry jam!
   And wonderful blackberry pie!

FLOPSY, MOPSY, COTTON-TAIL & MRS RABBIT: (*Sing.*)
   And blackberry tarts!
   And blackberry jelly!
   And blackberry jam!
   And wonderful blackberry pie!

(*PETER turns round and gives a sickly smile.*)

BEATRIX: And that is the end of the Tale of Peter Rabbit. We'll have an interval now of fifteen minutes so Peter can recover. And in the second half of the play you will meet Mrs Tiggy-Winkle and also Peter Rabbit's cousin, Benjamin Bunny!

PETER: (*Jumping up.*) And I'll be back too! Don't worry! (*To BEATRIX.*) Wasn't I brave? Will my name be in the papers? Do I get a medal?

BEATRIX: I haven't any medals – but here's a radish for you, Peter Rabbit.

(*BEATRIX presents PETER with a large radish.*)

PETER: Thank you, Miss Potter.

COMPANY: (*Sing.*)

> The green little, mean little, lean little berries
> Are always at the bottom of the blackberry bush.
> But the biggest best berries are always high
> On the branches way up in the sky.
> Though the brambles may scratch
> We jump and we hop
> For we have to snatch
> The ones at the top
> Yes the green little, mean little, lean little berries
> Are always at the bottom of the blackberry bush.
> But the biggest best berries are always high
> On the branches way up in the autumn sky.
> And those berries we'll cart
> Back home to our mam
> For blackberry tart
> And blackberry jam
> For the biggest best berries are always high
> On the branches way up in the autumn sky
> For blackberry tarts!
> And blackberry jelly!
> And blackberry jam!
> And wonderful blackberry pie!

BEATRIX: (*To AUDIENCE.*) We'll be back soon.

(*Exit COMPANY.*)

Interval.

ACT TWO

Enter BEATRIX and COMPANY.

BEATRIX: Peter Rabbit's still eating his nice fat radish. That should keep him quiet for a few minutes. Now we'd like to tell you – The Tale of Mrs Tiggy-Winkle.

PETER: And then another Rabbit story.

BEATRIX: Don't speak with your mouth full, Peter. Once upon a time there was a little girl called Lucie, who lived at a farm called Little-town.

PETER: Just a minute, just a minute, just a minute! I thought we were only going to do stories about animals. Little girls aren't animals!

BEATRIX: Have you ever met a little girl?

PETER: Well, not to speak to.

BEATRIX: Anyway. Lucie was a good little girl – only she was always losing her pocket-handkerchiefs. One day Lucie walked into the farmyard.

LUCIE: Oh, I've lost my pocket-handkin! Three handkins and a pinafore. Have you seen them, Tabby Kitten?

TABBY: (*Sings.*)
I'm washing my paws,
My little white paws,
I can't stop for handkins
And pinafores.

LUCIE: Sally Henny-Penny, have you found three pocket-handkerchiefs?

SALLY: (*Sings.*)
I'm scratching for worms
And grubs, if you please,
I can't stop for pinnies
And handkerchees.

LUCIE: Cock-Robin, have you seen my pinafore?

COCK-ROBIN: (*Sitting on stile, sings.*)
Lucie gives me breakfast toast
And biscuit crumbs for tea

If you want your pinafore
You'd better follow me!

(*COCK-ROBIN hops off the stile and flies away uphill.*)

LUCIE: He's flying right up the hill. Up – up – into the clouds round the hilltop. What's that up there? White things spread out on the grass? I'd better scramble up. This path's a bit steep. Big drop down that side. Oh, there's Little-town right away down below. I could drop a pebble down the chimney! (*She stops.*) Oh, here's a little spring, bubbling out of the hillside. It's like a tiny waterfall, daisies and speedwell all around. And some one's stood a tin can on a stone to catch the water. But the water's running over, for the can's no bigger than an egg-cup! I'd better follow this sandy path up the hill. I can see the foot-marks of a very small person.

(*LUCIE slows down to a standstill.*)

BEATRIX: The sandy path ended under a big rock. The grass was short and green, and there were clothes-lines made of plaited rushes and a heap of tiny clothes-pegs – but no pocket-handkerchiefs. But there was something else – a door! A door straight into the hill; and inside it somebody was singing.

TIGGY: (*Sings, off.*)

Lily-white and clean, oh!
With little frills between, oh!
Smooth and hot – red rusty spot
Never here be seen, oh!

(*LUCIE knocks at the door, twice.*)

TIGGY: (*Off, frightened.*) Who's that knocking at my door?

LUCIE I've never walked into a hill before. Here goes!

(*LUCIE opens the door and walks in. She is in a miniature farm kitchen – the ceiling is so low that LUCIE's head nearly touches it. There are small pots and pans and plates and everything.*)

There's a nice hot singey smell.

(*At the table, with an iron in her hand, stands a very stout, short person, MRS TIGGY-WINKLE. She stares anxiously at LUCIE. Her print gown is tucked up and she wears a*

*large apron over her striped petticoat. She has a little black
nose and twinkling eyes. TIGGY sniffs and sniffs.)*

TIGGY: Excuse my sniffling at you, if you please. But I
don't think we have met.

LUCIE: Excuse my staring at you. Most people have curls
underneath their caps, but your curls look more like –
um – prickles. Who are you? Have you seen my pocket-
handkerchiefs?

TIGGY: (*Curtsying.*) Oh, yes, if you please'm. My name is
Mrs Tiggy-Winkle. Oh, yes, if you please'm, I'm an
excellent clear-starcher and a washer and cleaner of all
sorts of garments.

(*TIGGY takes a piece of red cloth and starts to iron it.*)

LUCIE: That's not one of my pocket-handkins, is it?

TIGGY: Oh no, if you please'm; that's a little scarlet
waistcoat belonging to Cock Robin. (*She folds it, puts it
on one side and takes a bigger piece of cloth off a clothes-horse.*)

LUCIE: Is that my pinafore?

TIGGY: Oh no, if you please'm, that's a damask table-cloth
belonging to Jenny Wren. Look how it's stained with
currant wine! It's very bad to wash! Sniff, sniff! You sit
down, and I'll sniff around for your things.

(*LUCIE sits down while TIGGY slowly moves her nose around
in the air.*)

LUCIE: Oh, there's one of my pocket-handkins! And there's
my pinny!

TIGGY: (*Holding up the pinafore.*) I've ironed it and goffered
it. Now I shake out the frills.

LUCIE: Oh that is lovely! And what are those long yellow
things with fingers like gloves?

TIGGY: (*Holding them up.*) Oh this is a pair of stockings
belonging to Sally Henny-Penny – look how she's worn
the heels out with scratching in the yard! She'll very
soon have to scratch for worms in her bare feet!

LUCIE: Why, there's another handkersniff – but it isn't
mine – it's red.

TIGGY: Oh no, if you please'm. This one belongs to old
Mrs Rabbit; and it did so smell of onions! I've had to
wash it separately, I can't get out the smell.

(*PETER looks abashed.*)

LUCIE: There's another of mine. What are those funny little white things?

TIGGY: That's a pair of mittens. They belong to Tabby Kitten. I only have to iron them; she washes them herself. With her tongue.

LUCIE: There's my last pocket-handkin!

TIGGY: Now I've finished my ironing; I'm going to air some clothes.

LUCIE: What are those soft fluffy bits?

TIGGY: Woolly coats belonging to the little lambs at Skelghyl.

LUCIE: Do their jackets take off?

TIGGY: Oh, yes, if you please'm; look at the sheepmark on the shoulder. That shows which is whose and whose is which. Here's one marked for Gatesgarth and three from Little-town. They're always marked at washing! You can help me hang up the clothes if you've a mind to.

LUCIE: Yes please. (*They hang up clothes on pegs.*)

TIGGY: You could hang those little brown mouse-coats if you please.

LUCIE: (*Doing so.*) Who's this velvety waistcoat for?

TIGGY: That belongs to Doctor Mole.

LUCIE: And this red tail-coat with no tail?

TIGGY: Dear me, that's Squirrel Nutkin's. Do sit down by the fire. Would you like a cup of tea?

LUCIE: (*Sits on a bench by the fire.*) Yes please, Mrs Tiggy-Winkle.

(*TIGGY hands her a cup of tea and sits beside her.*
LUCIE, a little alarmed by her prickles, moves along the bench. They sip their cups.)

LUCIE: Are you magic, Mrs Tiggy-Winkle?

TIGGY: I don't hardly think so. But I do know a magic song. (*Sings.*)

> **This is the key of the kingdom:**
> **In that kingdom is a hill,**
> **On that hill there is a town,**
> **In that town there is a street,**
> **In that street there is a house,**

In that house there waits a room.
In that room there is a bed.
On that bed there is a basket,
A basket of bright flowers.
Bright flowers in the basket,
Basket on the bed,
Bed inside the room,
Room inside the house,
House in the winding street,
Street in the high town,
Town in the kingdom,
Town in the kingdom:
This is the key of the kingdom.

Now, if you've finished your tea, let's put the clothes in bundles. Here, I'll fold your pocket-handkerchiefs inside your clean pinny. And fasten 'em up with a silver safety-pin. You take that bundle, I'll take the rest. Come on. (*Leads the way out of the door.*) There, I always locks the door and hides the key under this old tortoise stone. Let's trot down the hill together.
(*TIGGY and LUCIE start out on their way.*)

BEATRIX: All the way down the path little animals came out of the fern to meet them.
(*Out pops PETER RABBIT.*)

PETER: Have you seen my little blue jacket with shiny buttons, Mrs Tiggy-Winkle?

TIGGY: No, but I'll keep an eye open for it, Peter Rabbit, you rascal!

PETER: Very much obliged to you, dear Mrs Tiggy-Winkle.
(*COCK-ROBIN, HENNY-PENNY, MRS TITTLE-MOUSE, MRS RABBIT and TABBY KITTEN claim their clothes, till there's nothing left to carry except LUCIE's little bundle.*)

ANIMALS: (*Leaving.*) Thank you! That's lovely! Thank you, Mrs Tiggy-Winkle!

LUCIE: It's getting dark. I'd better be off home to Little-town. (*Climbs over the stile and turns.*) Good night – where's she gone? Mrs Tiggy-Winkle! I haven't thanked you. And I haven't paid you for the washing. There she goes. Running running up the hill. But where's her frilly cap? And her gown? And her petticoat? And how small she's grown! And how brown she's grown! And she's all covered with prickles! Ah, now I see. Mrs Tiggy-Winkle was nothing but a Hedgehog!

(*It is night and the full moon shines. MRS TIGGY-WINKLE and other ANIMALS enter to sing with LUCIE.*)

COMPANY: (*Sing.*)

> **When the dew falls silently**
> **And stars begin to twinkle,**
> **Underneath the hollow tree**
> **Peeps Mrs Tiggy-winkle.**
> **When the sheep are fast asleep,**
> **Her little brown eyes twinkle –**
> **And a glow-worm lights the way**
> **For Mrs Tiggy-winkle.**
> **Where the whispering waters pass**
> **In brooks that jump and tinkle,**
> **Up and down the dewy grass**
> **Trots Mrs Tiggy-winkle.**

BEATRIX: And now it's time for our last story – The Tale of Benjamin Bunny.

BENJAMIN: (*Sings.*)

> **I'm Benjamin Bunny**
> **My nature is sunny**
> **I'm brave as a rabbit can be**
> **As I jump through the grass**
> **All the creatures I pass**
> **Point me out**
> **And they shout**
> **Who is he?**

ANIMALS: (*Sing.*)

> **Who is he?**
> **Who is he?**
> **Who is he?**

BENJAMIN: (*Sings.*)

> **I'm Benjamin Bunny**
> **My jokes are all funny**

I'm happy and fit as a flea
As I run and I leap
All the cows and the sheep
Point me out
And they shout
Who is he?
ANIMALS: (*Sing.*)
Who is he?
Who is he?
Who is he?
BENJAMIN: (*Sings.*)
I'm Benjamin Bunny
Benjamin Bunny
Benjamin Bunny
That's me!
PETER: I could be the hero of this one too. I could dress
up as Benjamin –
BEATRIX: No, Peter, Benjamin can act himself.
(*BEATRIX turns away and bends down to pick up her paints.*
PETER, piqued, picks up a large stick of celery.)
PETER: It's not fair, Miss Potter.
(*He whacks BEATRIX on the bottom with the celery stick.*
All ANIMALS gasp – what has he done?
BEATRIX straightens up but does not turn to face us yet.)
TIGGY: (*Finally riled.*) Master Peter, you'll stop being rude
to Miss Potter. If she hadn't writ those stories and drawed
those pictures, nobody would ever have heard of you.
Mind your manners, or I'll make myself into a spiky ball
and roll all over you.
PETER: (*Chastened, handing BEATRIX the celery stick.*) Sorry,
Miss Potter, I got carried away.
BEATRIX: (*Turning, suppressing her giggles.*) That's all right,
Peter.
BENJAMIN: I'll let you be in my story, Peter.
PETER: Huzzah! It can begin with me writing a letter.
(*PETER sits to compose a letter, writing with a pheasant*
feather pen which he dips into an inkpot.)
PETER: (*As he writes.*) To Mr McGregor, Gardener's
Cottage. Dear Sir, I write to ask whether your spring

cabbages are ready? Kindly reply by return and oblige yours truly, Peter Rabbit.

(*PETER shakes ink from his pen on to the letter, pops it in an envelope and gives it to ROBIN REDBREAST who hops over to MRS MCGREGOR.*)

MRS McGREGOR: (*Taking the letter.*) Nasty day, isn't it, Robin Redbreast?

(*ROBIN shrugs.*

MRS McGREGOR reads letter in half a second, then writes furiously.)

To Master P Rabbit, Under The Fir Tree. Sir, I write by desire of my husband Mr McGregor who is bed with a cold to say if you comes here again we will inform the Polisse. Jane McGregor. PS. I have bought a new pie-dish. It is very large. PPS Mr McGregor's cold is worsened so I take him to the doctor today in the pony-cart.

(*ROBIN takes her letter back to PETER, who glances at it and writes another letter in one brief scribble. ROBIN takes it over to where BENJAMIN BUNNY sits, chewing a leaf.*)

BENJAMIN: (*Reading.*) "To Master Benjamin Bunny, The Warren." (*Sits up straight.*) That's me! I never had a letter before. Let's see. "Dear Cousin Benjamin, I have had a very badly written letter from Mrs McGregor, she says she and Mr McGregor are off to the doctor's. Will you watch the road and come tell me when they are gone? In haste, your affectionate cousin, Peter Rabbit."

(*There is a sound of a pony and trap.*)

That sounds like the McGregors! I see them, I see them. Mrs McGregor's wearing her best bonnet. And Mr McGregor's looking like a sickly old goat. Huzzah!

(*BENJAMIN sets off with a hop, skip and jump to call on PETER.*

Sings.)

Running down the path
For to visit my cousins –
Flopsy,
Mopsy,

Cotton-tail
And Peter.
They live with their mother in a sand-bank
Underneath the roots of a big fir-tree –
Flopsy,
Mopsy,
Cotton-tail
And Peter.

BENJAMIN: (*Stopping, and looking around.*) But I don't very much want to see my Aunt, Peter's Mother. I'll creep round the back of the fir-tree. (*He trips and nearly falls on top of PETER who sits by himself, looking ill and dressed in a red cotton pocket-handkerchief. Whispers.*) Peter.
(*PETER sneezes.*)
Peter! You do look poorly. Why are you wrapped in that red cotton handkerchief? Who has got your clothes?

PETER: The scarecrow in Mr McGregor's garden.

BENJAMIN How did that happen?
(*PETER is suddenly animated, jumps up, and at great speed gives a fast-forward version of his adventures, acting out as much of the action as possible but trying to appear heroic.*)

PETER: (*At top speed.*) Flopsy, Mopsy and Cottontail were picking some silly blackberries so I broke into Mr McGregor's garden and ate half his vegetables but then I nearly bumped into Mr McGregor so I led him a merry dance but my jacket got caught in a horrible net but I wriggled out of it and hid cunningly in a watering can but it was full of water so I scared his cat so much its fur turned white and then I jumped out over the gate leaving Mr McGregor flabbergastered and flummoxed.

BENJAMIN: You're a very brave rabbit, Peter. Anyway, I saw the McGregors on their way to the doctor in the pony-cart.

PETER: D'you think they'll be away all day?

BENJAMIN: Oh yes. She was wearing her best bonnet. She'll be shopping and gossiping all around the market.

MRS RABBIT: (*Off.*) Cotton-tail! Cotton-tail! Fetch some more camomile!

PETER: I think I might feel better if I went for a walk.
(*PETER and BENJAMIN walk and climb on the flat top of a wall.*)

BENJAMIN: From here you can see right down into Mr McGregor's garden. Look! Carrot-tops and fresh young cabbages and lots of little lettuces.

PETER: (*Still wrapped in the handkerchief.*) Yes – and there's my fine blue coat and shoes on that scarecrow.

BENJAMIN: But what's the scarecrow wearing on its turnip-head?

PETER: That looks like an old tam-o-shanter of Mr McGregor's. Let's squeeze under the gate.

BENJAMIN: It spoils people's clothes to squeeze under gates. The proper way to get in, is to climb down a pear tree.
(*BENJAMIN and PETER climb down a tree into the garden. PETER falls and rolls over, feigning dead.*)

BENJAMIN: Are you all right, Peter?

PETER: (*Laughing.*) Yes, the flower bed's all new raked – it's soft as feathers.

BENJAMIN: (*Inspecting with the eye of an expert.*) These seeds are going to be lettuces!

PETER Well, try not to squash them with your great clogs!

BENJAMIN: (*Approaching the scarecrow.*) The first thing to do is to get back your clothes. I need that pocket-handkerchief.
(*BENJAMIN and PETER strip the scarecrow of tam-o-shanter, coat and shoes. PETER puts on the jacket first, then the shoes.*)

PETER: (*Trying on shoes.*) Ooh! They're full of water.

BENJAMIN: Of course – it rained last night. (*Puts on the tam-o-shanter.*) A very nice warm hat.

PETER: (*Laughing.*) It's ten times too big for you.

BENJAMIN: Well, you try it, turnip-head!
(*BENJAMIN throws the tammy at PETER, who dodges. They let the tammy lie on the ground.*)

BENJAMIN: Come on. Fill your handkerchief with onions. They can be a little present for your mother.

PETER: Yes. (*Nervously jumping up.*) What was that? Did that sound like a pony-cart to you?

BENJAMIN: No, I just dropped an onion. Come and help.

PETER: Of course. I – I saw a flash of something on the road.

BENJAMIN: (*Chewing a lettuce leaf.*) Only a couple of magpies landing. Two for joy. Have a lettuce leaf?

PETER: (*Nervously.*) Not just now, thanks.

BENJAMIN: I often drop in to the garden of a Saturday to collect a few lettuces for our Sunday dinner. Very fine lettuces, they are. What was that song you taught me, Peter?

BENJAMIN: (*Sings noisily.*)

Let us have a lettuce,
Munch, munch, munch.
Next I'll chew a carrot,
Crunch, crunch, crunch.
Then I'll have a radish,
To finish my lunch.
For I'm sure that Mr McGregor's not here today.
Yes I'm sure that Mr McGregor has gone away
So –
Let us have a lettuce,
Munch, munch, munch.
Next I'll chew a carrot,
Crunch, crunch, crunch.
Then I'll have a radish,
To finish my lunch.

PETER: Not so loud, Benjamin. I think I'd like to go home now. Oh! (*He drops half the onions out of the handkerchief.*)

BENJAMIN: Butterfingers!

PETER: Shall we climb the pear-tree?

BENJAMIN: Can't manage that with a load of onions. Follow me.

(*BENJAMIN marches boldly down the garden, followed by PETER, who keeps looking around.*)

PETER Those mice by the cucumber-frame – they winked at us!

BENJAMIN Don't mind them.
(PETER is a step or two ahead, he suddenly stops and turns.)
BENJAMIN: What's the matter, Peter? Your eyes are as big as lolly-pops!
PETER: Look. It's the white cat.
BENJAMIN: Don't scare her, Peter, or she'll raise the alarm. Just slip underneath this basket.
(BENJAMIN lifts up one side of a wicker basket and he and PETER hide under it with the onions.
The WHITE CAT gets up, stretches, then comes and sniffs the basket.)
WHITE CAT: Oooh! Onions. I do enjoy the smell of onions.
(WHITE CAT settles down on the basket.)
BEATRIX You can't see Peter and Benjamin underneath the basket. I'd draw you a picture of them, but the smell of onions is too fearful. The onion-smell is making Peter and Benjamin cry.
WHITE CAT: *(Sings.)*
> **The white cat sat**
> **And sat and sat**
> **And sat and sat and sat**
> **Onions on the ground**
> **Rabbits on the onions**
> **Basket on the rabbits**
> **And all the afternoon**
> **On top of that basket**
> **The white cat sat**
> **And sat and sat**
> **And sat and sat and sat!**

BEATRIX: She sat on the basket for FIVE HOURS! But then there was a pitter-patter, pitter-patter from the top of the garden wall. The cat looked up and saw old Mr Benjamin Bunny prancing along the wall.
(Enter MR BUNNY, smoking a pipe of rabbit-tobacco.)
MR BUNNY: *(To the WHITE CAT.)* I'm looking for my son, young Benjamin. Have you seen hide or fur of him?
WHITE CAT: *(Snarling.)* This is a private garden. No rabbits allowed.

MR BUNNY: Who says so?

WHITE CAT: I say so. I am the garden cat.

MR BUNNY: Well I am old Mr Benjamin Bunny, and I have no opinion whatever of cats.

(MR BUNNY jumps from the wall onto the WHITE CAT and cuffs it off the basket and kicks it off the stage. A rumbustious fight follows in which PETER and BENJAMIN are scratched by the WHITE CAT and accidentally bumped by MR BUNNY. The WHITE CAT, who has never been treated like this before, retreats in terror into the greenhouse. MR BUNNY shuts and locks the door behind her. She watches through the greenhouse window.)

MR BUNNY: Benjamin and Peter – I hope you've learned your lesson. (*They nod dolefully.*) Quick march!

(MR BUNNY picks up the handkerchief of onions and marches BENJAMIN and PETER out of the garden.)

BEATRIX: When Mr McGregor returned about half an hour later, he observed several things which puzzled him.

(Enter MR McGREGOR, walking thoughtfully around his garden.)

MR MCGREGOR: It looks as though somebody has been walking all over my garden in a pair of clogs – only the foot-marks are ridiculously little! And (*Unlocking the greenhouse door and letting out the miaowing WHITE CAT.*) – how did you manage to shut yourself inside my greenhouse and lock the door on the outside. It's a mystery to baffle Sherlock Holmes himself!

(BENJAMIN nods goodbye as PETER enters his home. MRS RABBIT hugs PETER.)

PETER: I'm sorry, Mother – I've been –

MRS RABBIT: I know – you've been into that garden. But I forgive you. I'm so glad you found your shoes and coat. Now we can hang those lovely onions from the kitchen ceiling with the bunches of herbs and rabbit-tobacco.

COMPANY (Sing.)
That's a happy ending
For Benjamin Bunny

And
Flopsy,
Mopsy,
Cotton-tail
And Peter.
Who live with their mother in a sand-bank
Underneath the roots of a big fir-tree –
Flopsy,
Mopsy,
Cotton-tail
And Peter.

BEATRIX: When I was very small
The town was very big
My only friends were a wooden doll
And a grimy little cotton pig.
But when I was taken to the countryside, I made
hundreds of animal friends. Now you've met some of
them, so they're your friends too. You can read about
them in my books and act out their stories at school or
at home. And I hope that you'll always have lots of
animal and human friends of your own. Now, before we
say goodbye, we'd like to remind you of a few of our
songs!
(*Medley.*
To be chosen when the tunes have been rehearsed, to reflect
something of each of the four stories. During the medley,
animals proudly show their pictures which BEATRIX has
been painting. At the end of the Medley BEATRIX, LUCIE
and all the ANIMALS wave goodbye to the AUDIENCE.)

Peter Rabbit and His Friends

Songs

ACT ONE

1. WHEN I WAS VERY SMALL – Beatrix Potter and Company
2. THOMASINA TITTLEMOUSE – Beatrix and Company
3. LADYBIRD, LADYBIRD – Mrs Tittlemouse
4. IPSEY WIPSEY SPIDER – Ipsey and Mrs Tittlemouse
5. TIDDLY, WIDDLY, WIDDLY – Bees and Mr Jackson
6. NID, NID, NODDY – Company
7. I CAN'T SIT STILL – Peter Rabbit and Company
8. FLOPSY, MOPSY – Mrs Rabbit and Beatrix
9. BLACKBERRIES – Flopsy, Mopsy and Cotton-Tail
10. RABBIT LUNCH – Peter
11. ANIMAL LOVER – Mr McGregor
12. WHITE CAT – White Cat
13. BLACKBERRIES (reprise) – Flopsy, Mopsy, Cotton-tail and Mrs Rabbit

ACT TWO

1. CAN'T STOP – Tabby Kitten and Sally Henny-Penny
2. FOLLOW ME – Cock-Robin
3. LILY-WHITE – Mrs Tiggy-Winkle
4. THE KEY OF THE KINGDOM – Mrs Tiggy-Winkle
5. MRS TIGGY-WINKLE – Company
6. I'M BENJAMIN BUNNY – Benjamin Bunny and Animals
7. FLOPSY, MOPSY (reprise) – Benjamin
8. RABBIT LUNCH (reprise) – Benjamin
9. THE WHITE CAT SAT – White Cat
10. FLOPSY, MOPSY (reprise) – Company
    MEDLEY